HOW TO BE A SINCERE PHONEY

"Oklahoma dust that enriched Will Rogers
settled also on Jim Boren. ...They shared a common
heritage, sought the same truths and used similar tools.
...They blazed uncanny trails of truth made hospitable by
mirth and humor. Get a belly ache from laughter."

JOE CARTER, Will Rogers biographer
Director, Will Rogers Museum

I dedicate this book...

To the honest and courageous public officials and
private citizens who fight for honesty, truth, and integrity in
government service, and especially among them,

Norma...
for the brilliance of her teaching,
the brightness of her spirit,
the music of her laughter,
the goodness of her heart, and
the exciting magic of her love,

and

Opal and the late U.S. Senator Ralph Yarborough...
for the many years of warm and inspiring friendship,
and for proving that honesty, truth, and integrity
can prevail in a lifetime of outstandingly
competent public service in behalf of the people.

HOW TO BE A SINCERE PHONEY

A handbook for politicians and bureaucrats

JAMES H. BOREN, PhD

BIRDCAGE Publications
and
EPM Custom Books

Library of Congress Cataloging in Publication Data

Boren, James H.
    How to be a sincere phoney: A handbook for politicians
and bureaucrats / James H. Boren
      p. cm.
    ISBN 1-889324-17-5
    1. Bureaucracy Humor. 2. Politicians Humor. I. Title.
JF 1501.B67 1999
324.2'2'0207—dc21

                    99-34092
                    CIP

Printed in Canada
Copyright ® 1999 James H.Boren
All Rights Reserved
Birdcage Publications
    One Plaza South , Tahlequah, OK 74464
and EPM Custom Books
    4138 Fox Hollow Rd., Delaplane, VA 20144
    (800) 289-2339

Text Cartoons by Bill Rechin
Cover Design by Tom Huestis

ACKNOWLEDGMENTS

I am in debt to many people who gave encouragement and sagacious advice as I began to write this book. My beloved wife, Norma, who encouraged me with words, cornbread, uninterrupted time, Irish coffee, and shared orbitations of ideas.

Bill Rechin is not only an outstanding syndicated cartoonist, he is also a close friend with whom I have shared many joyous mumbles as we have collaborated on various endeavors. As illustrator and cartoonist for this book, his ingenious mind and zappy pen continue to reveal a master at work.

Joe Carter, a long-time friend who has always encouraged me along the humor trail; Ed Brocksmith and Ed Fite, friends and valiant fighters for the preservation of the beloved, scenic Illinois River; Lowell Lehman, great master of all music, the writer of the Postmaster General March: Semper Defunctus which was recorded by the U.S. Naval Academy Band; U. S. Senator Jim Inhofe who looked at the pictures in one of my books, and who inspired the title for this one;

Art Cox, my friend who is a steadfast and cynical evaluator of things nonpartisan; Blake Purdy who, as the Chief Pilot of Bentwing Airlines, flew a 1941 J3 Piper Cub as security patrol for our 35-acre Tick Ranch;

Supportive Financiers Mark Gish, Edwin and Helen Lynch; Lloyd Spyres, protector of my back as I did conceptual research for this book at council meetings;

Roger Webb, Larry Williams, Lyle Haskins, Brian Rader, Jim Walker and other helpful colleagues who made academe a friendly and stimulating world at Northeastern State University; B. J. Medley, Ben Odom, Joel Carson, Joel Bendorf, Jack LaFevers, Tim Mauldin, Dan Lowe, Rolly Lowe, Wayne Salisbury, the late Bill Reynolds and many others who have shared battles with me in the political domain; Russian writers Oleg and Andrey Benyukh, Alexei Pyanov, Cartoonist Vladimir Mochalev; the late Laurence J. Peter, my friend of shared travel and joyous mumbles; Barbara Wade, Biblical Advisor.

Evelyn Metzger, wonderful publisher of past books, who served as my mentor and editorial guidance system for this book; Tom Huestis, gifted designer of the book's covers; Vance Gibson, friend, artist, and photographer.

The family of the inspiring J. W. Hamilton (who taught me about chickens), Dick, Stan, Cathy, Catie, Todd, James, John, Brother Gene, Sister Marilyn.

I wish also to acknowledge the encouragement given by my shipmates of the USS William C. Cole, John Cosgrove and other friends of the Destroyer Escort Sailors Association with whom I sailed during WWII;

Of course, I acknowledge the work of a few faceless bureaucrats and the many nameless politicians who served as models and enlightening facsimiles of public servants in the Great Valley of the Potomac.

CONTENTS

INTRODUCTION

Oklahoma dust that enriched Will rogers settled also on Jim Boren. Oklahoma heat that embroiled Will Rogers to ignite humorous embers under sweaty politicos also fired the imagination of Jim Boren. As a Will Rogers biographer and an ancient friend of Jim Boren, parallels between these two humorists seem obvious. They shared a common heritage, sought the same truths and used similar tools.

Jim Boren and Will Rogers both adroitly harnessed humor to lope into the deeper mysteries and myths of humanity but particularly to expose the political system. They wrote and they spoke. They cajoled. They cast light into the inner sanctums.

Laughter, chuckles and guffaws crackle from both of their writings. When either spoke, folks in the audience more appropriately would gently push an elbow into a nearby rib and whisper: "You know, he's right."

From the hills of Oklahoma to the halls of Congress and tunneling Washington bureaucracies, Will Rogers and Jim Boren blazed uncanny trails of truth made hospitable by mirth and humor.

Read Will Rogers. Read Jim Boren. Study them.

Accept digestible truths. Learn carefully because truth is dangerous. Get a belly ache from laughter.

Joe Carter, Director
Will Rogers Museum,
President, Will Rogers Heritage Trust
Claremore, Oklahoma

HOW TO READ THIS BOOK

How to be a Sincere Phoney is not a book to be read in a single evening. Single-evening reading could be dangerous to your health... mental and physical. It's to be read a chapter or two at a time. You may gag at some of the reality underlying its satirical message, or your blood pressure may soar on wings of disgust and anger. On the other hand, your gastroenterologist may suggest a longer reading the night before a colonoscopy. Whatever your personal response may be, I hope there will be enough smiles and knowing nods of the head to leave you with pleasure at having read the book. More important, I hope you become more involved in the peoples' business of governing ourselves.

HOW TO USE THIS BOOK

IF YOU ARE A BUREAUCRAT OR A POLITICIAN, YOU CAN USE THIS BOOK...

<u>As a handbook of confidence</u>. Keep it on your
desk; carry it in your briefcase; place it on your night-
stand or within reach from your favorite chair; use it as a
centerpiece at the breakfast table; set one near the throne
in your bathroom. It should be available as an authoritative reference book and a comforting book of encouragement wherever you may be. Knowing that it is at hand
will help you gain confidence in yourself, and you will
find a sense of well-being through knowing "It is there."

<u>As a guide to career enhancement</u>. If you are a
fledgling bureaucrat or wannabe politician, study the lessons in the book as the bureaucrats' bible that can help you
bubble in a cesspoolian movement to the upper crust of
your organization. Concentrate on the strategies and language of each chapter, and watch the old pros around you
as they use them throughout each day. Begin to use the
techniques yourself, and as you gain confidence, adapt
them to your own style.

If you are already an established and accomplished
bureaucrat or an elected official, use the book to expand
the philosophy and perfect the techniques that have
brought you to a professional level. Make the collection
of Borenwords a matter of regular reading until you can
mumble the words with flowing eloquence and adjustive
resonance. Expand your vocabulary and decrease your
vulnerability by learning to mumble, fuzzify, profundify,
globate, and drivelate.

IF YOU ARE NOT A BUREAUCRAT OR A POLITI-
CIAN, BUT IF YOU MUST DEAL WITH THOSE WHO
ARE, YOU CAN USE THIS BOOK...

As an aid to survival. Many non-bureaucrats know
what is being done to them, but they rarely understand
why and how it is being done. Learn to recognize a mumble when you hear one and a sincere phoney when you see
one. Understand the cozy accommodation that has been
established between the legislative branch and the bureaucracy, between the executive offices and the board of
directors, or between the Administration and the Board of
Regents.

Know when a corporate bureaucrat is giving you
the shuffle in the hope you will not follow up on a legiti-
mate beef. Arrogantual insurance companies and HMO's
become strong and rich by reaping huge profits from those
they serve (or service?) through dynamic inaction, doing
nothing but doing it with style.'

Learn the difference between a fail-safe educator
and one who makes learning relevant and exciting. Know
when you are being ripped off by a nitpicker or a yes-but-
ter. Grasp the real purpose of a chief executive who
appoints a blue ribbon commission or a task force. By
elimination, learn to identify the bureaucrat or politician
who really wants to do his or her job ... and knows how to
do it. And understand full well that there are as many
excesses and deficiencies in corporate and academic
bureaucracies as government.

As a basis for self-evaluation. Have you drifted
into the bureaucratic swamp without being aware of it?
Do you ponder when you are in charge, delegate when you

are in trouble, and mumble when you are in doubt? Do you fuzzify your goals and profundify simplicity? Have you patted someone on the back as a means of locating their wallet or evaluate other resources? Have you wasted someone's competence today? Do you postpone trouble-some problems in the hope the problems will go away? Do you discourage creativity among your associates or subordinates, because innovation may disturb the comfort-able status quo? Do you publicly criticize others for doing what you privately do yourself? Do you produce, or require others to produce, more paperwork than is neces-sary? Do you practice dynamic inaction? Are you a suf-fering victim of bureaucracy of political action who shouts and cries but who never fights back? Are you a part of the social drift?

DISCOVERING A NEW WAY OF LIFE

In 1968, after fighting bureaucracy in all walks of life, I experienced a sudden conversion during a senior-level staff meeting in the State Department. It was the discovery that there can be inspiration in dynamic inaction... doing nothing but doing it with style. It was the revelation that there can be beauty in a bag of mush, poetry in nondirective language, and music in the fuzzistic mumble of marginal thoughts. I began organizing the world's first Bureaucratic Movement dedicated to the cause of mmablksgintionlumumble. INATAPROBU now has members in 17 nations.

With the exception of a brief period in 1996, when I fought a losing battle against a U.S. Senator in the political realm of aggressive ignorance and fiscal snuggling, I have served as a missionary striving to preserve and strengthen the bureaucratic way of life.

After extensive experience in business, academe, politics, the U.S. Foreign Service, and travel in fifty-eight nations of the world, I have learned some lessons about the bureaucratic way of life that I feel impelled to share with others who may wish to survive and thrive in the world's magnificent bureaucracies. I have brought together many of those lessons as well as some of my more recent nondirective thoughts to help others find the peace and happiness of bureaucratic salvation.

To enter into the bureaucratic kingdom is to find security from the harsh realities of the world at play or war, and to enjoy the status of importance without responsibility. It is to gain respect from unknowing underlings, and to possess the image of power that can rule over those who are the fearful or timid nonchallengers of bureaucracy. Many years ago, as a beginning high school teacher, I sought whatever guidance I could find that would help me perform my duties in an effective and professional way. I studied scholarly books, I read professional journals, and I gathered marginal pearls of wisdom from other classroom practitioners. It was not until after several years of experience, however, that I learned that the educational process is often one that transforms active bodies and inquiring minds into settled bodies and dormant minds. It can be a process which reflects the same orbital transformation found among most members of the governing school boards. Experience has taught me that the excitement of learning is, at best, a byproduct of the essential educational processes of maintaining records, completing mandated reports, keeping a quiet classroom, organizing a pretty bulletin board and assuring that venetian blinds are at the same level to improve the appearance of the school to passing taxpayers. As a beginning teacher, I made many mistakes. I had no list of helpful hints on how to become an accepted member of the academic team.

I recall, for example, being berated by my colleagues, because I broke the travels of "the moving eraser." One day, as I was teaching my class at Oxnard Union High School, a student entered my room, and handed me a chalky eraser with the message, "Mr. Miller sent this to you." I was puzzled. I had plenty of erasers. Why would my friend, Bob, send me an eraser? I added it to the collection on the tray at the bottom of the chalk board. But I had broken the chain of communications. The eraser should have been passed on to the next classroom. No one had told me that "the moving eraser" meant that the superintendent of the school system was on the prowl - visiting classes on an unannounced basis. I had failed my first test as a member of the faculty, and my failure was due to my need for practical guidance about one of the most important aspects of secondary education.

Similarly, as an employee of municipal, state and national governmental agencies, I learned that there were no readily available guidelines or practical suggestions to help me learn how to accomplish my task or build an image of success. In one of my first jobs as the night director of a city recreation center, I found that my most effective management decision evolved from a frantic and desperate effort to maintain order in the place. I put on boxing gloves and went a few rounds with three young tough leaders whose respect and friendship were later helpful in running the center.

Later, at the quasi-executive pigeon-level under the dome of the state capitol in Austin, Texas, I learned new lessons. I learned not only how to fill out forms but also how to juggle budgetary items, develop overlapping reports, harmonize conflicting travel vouchers, and issue checks. Without the helpful guidance from the old timers in the accounting office, one of the state auditors, and the three top bosses, I would have wandered unknowingly among the pigeons even longer than I did.

As the state campaign manager and, later, the Administrative Assistant to U.S. Senator Ralph Yarborough in Washington, I learned how to get things done, a productive skill on Capitol Hill but a subversive art in the "downtown" bureaucracies. The Senator wanted results, and I learned how to produce. This pattern of productive work was to be a problem for me in my later career. The change from productive action to orbital and image-oriented movement, I was to learn, is as difficult to achieve as a golfer to "unlearn" bad techniques acquired through years of duffing on the course or hitting thousands of buckets of balls at a driving range.

It was as a senior level foreign service officer that I came into my own. I began with the usual search for guidance from men and women experienced in international affairs. I learned one bit of philosophy in one place, a marginal technique in another, and a few procedural abstractions in still another. I learned that international affairs were the same as domestic affairs except for the jargon and the dizzying mystique of dealing with diplomats... ours and others. Gradually, I had accumulated a loose bundle of concepts and skills that helped me meander meaningfully from day to day.

In late March of 1968, I was sitting in one of the chairs ringing the executive conference room on the sixth floor of the State Department Building. The weekly staff meeting, under the direction of the Assistant Secretary for InterAmerican Affairs, had begun like so many such meetings before. Each person at the table took his or her turn in either reporting on some problem or development (real or imagined) that had occurred during the preceding week, or with a mumbled "Nothing today", passed the semantical ball to the occupant of the next chair. After the table-sitters performed, those in the wall-hugging chairs followed suit.

The meeting was not different from those I had attended for five years - except for one significant thing. It was a meeting of great personal discovery! I was quietly puffing on my large-bowled, conservative pipe, and watch-

17

ing the semantical toss from chair occupant to chair occupant. It was a dull and boring meeting. I twiggled my toes and counted my teeth with my tongue to stay awake. My molar=checking was interrupted when suddenly I observed something I had not seen before. Though the boobidoodles on the note pads were the same, and though the countenances of my colleagues were the typical meeting-gray, I saw a spark of excitement in the eyes of each semanticizer in the double circles as the toss was made.

My head snapped to attention, and I coughed on an extra puff of my pipe. Why was there a sparkle in the eyes of each participant as he or she performed? I watched with a searching gaze on each pair of eyes as the mumbled messages were mangled. Then it happened! It was the gestalt - the configuration pattern was completed - the pieces came together - the "Aha, I see it now" phenomenon flashed to completion. I was watching my colleagues as they were devitalizing ideas with deft thrusts of yesbuttisms and forthright twiddlisms. They were speaking of viable options and action plans while actually formulating inaction concepts. "Eureka!" I though, "this is fantastic! Dynamic inaction!

I had discovered there can be inspiration in dynamic inaction... doing nothing but doing it with style. What a beautiful bag of mush! Poetic sounds that wandered around the room with clunkal pentameters looking for a significant thought! Music in incoherent mumbles of marginal concepts!

I trembled with excitement as I watched the few remaining performers make their semantical tosses. I even forgot to stoke my pipe for the balance of the meeting. I sat on the edge of my chair trying to capture each Ivy League mumble and each lobing of the eyes... the radarlike sweep of the room.

When the meeting ended, I frantically (but with dignity) shuffled around the table in search of any boobidoodled notes that may have been abandoned. It was a fruitless search, of course, because nearly all bureaucrats solemnly fold and pocket their "notes of the meeting." "Never mind," I thought, "just wait 'til next week." I shuffled my way into the marble hall in the vain hope of gathering any last minute sparks from the solemn parade - the bureaucratic flow of bodies at attention and minds at ease.

Dynamic inaction! Doing nothing but doing it with style. I kept repeating the concept in my mind. What had I been missing all of these years? Why hadn't someone clued me in? Safety but participation. Zilch but zilch with class. Wow!

Then I began to ask myself questions. How many others in the world were sitting through boring meetings, rumperatorily shifting position in their chairs, and slipping quick glances at the creeping hands of their watches? How many others were molar-checking and twiggling as they sought to stay awake in staff meetings, conferences or religious services? How many other bureaucrats were awaiting the day of discovery - waiting to be invited to the rail of bureaucratic salvation? How many other careers were ready for enrichment and enhancement?

As I slowly but happily strolled toward my office, I realized that I had a new mission in life. I had to share my discovery with others. I had to teach others to keep the erasers of the world moving from one haven to another. I stopped by a window to gaze with glaze at the huge building housing the U.S. Office of Personnel Management. "Yes," I thought, "I must open the doors to the world of dynamic inaction and lead others to its harbors of peace, tranquility, and thrivality. I must become a missionary in the cause of creative nonresponsiveness.

Within three weeks of my discovery and the decision to do good works, I held a press conference in the President's Room of The National Press Club. To the media representatives, I announced my plan to found The National Association of Professional Bureaucrats (NATAPROBU). As the message oozed across national borders, the response was so overwhelming and widespread that the original idea of a national association was quickly expanded to one of international dimensions. Thus was born the International Association of Professional Bureaucrats... INATAPROBU, and my work in dynamic inaction, decision postponement, orbital dialoguing, and creative mumbling.

In my travels around the world, I began to observe what I thought was a strange relationship that existed among bureaucrats and politicians. With more travel and deeper study into the institutional orbits of each nation, I began to distinguish among the bureaucrats and politicians in Brazil where bureaucracy is a great art form. In the former Soviet Union, there were no distinctions between the two, and since the clunkational interfacing of glosnost and peristroika, the amalgamation became even more solidified into a new Mother Russia. In Italy, the fusion was one of joyous embraces and multiphonic orations. In Germany, bureaucracy and politics exhibited an adhesion of profound solemnity. In Great Britain and Canada, the parliamentary system was the basis of formal merger. When I began to study my own country, I learned what should have been obvious to me at the beginning. Politicians are a special kind of bureaucrat, and the most successful bureaucrats are politicians.

Why had I been so slow to realize this simple fact

of life? I pondered with ineffable prodigiosity. At last, I concluded that my years of total immersion in the dynamic inaction of bureaucracy had caused my brain to function in slushmentalized comfort. My devotion to the bureaucratic way of life had given me a microseptic view of institutional harmonics. Now, however, I knew I had to go forth into the real world of a politicratic power... where politicians and bureaucrats share and perform with quiet camaraderie. Politicians could publicly blast the faceless bureaucrats when speaking in their domain, yet give them the power to govern through the generality of legislation. The politicians would avoid facing difficult political decisions by passing broad brush legislation, then delegating to the bureaucrats the authority "to promulgate such rules and regulations as may be necessary to carry out the purposes of the Act."

Eureka! The world is truly ours. Politicians and bureaucrats are brothers and sisters... one great family with common interests, shared goals, and mutual private devotion. And our needs are common; survival, thrival, and power. This book seeks to share the marginal wisdom of an old practitioner of the politicratic arts with those who would succeed as bureaucrats or politicians. Study each concept and practice with care. And read between the lines.

Jim Boren

PART ONE.

Jim Boren Advisories

Attitude adjustment before plunging into the book

Part One. JIM BOREN ADVISORIES

1. Never argue with stupid people who may know more than you do.

2. Sharing ignorance may not lead to wisdom, but it spreads responsibility.

3. It's hard to look up to a leader who keeps his ear to the ground.

4. When a politician or a bureaucrat makes a mistake and continues to make it, it usually becomes the new policy.

5. Bureaucracy is the epoxy that greases the wheels of progress.

6. If your position on an issue proves to be wrong, don't change your position, redefine the issue.

7. Forgetting the right things is better than remembering the wrong things.

8. Lawnmowers don't cut grass; people do.

9. When a lobbyist and a politician play loophole golf, the score is determined by the size and shape of the loophole and the number of strokes on the palm of the politician. The taxpayers furnish the greens.

10. Subsidies, tax loopholes, and defense contracts are the accepted ways of redistributing the wealth among those with the most clout.

11. Ignorance never stops politicians from saying what they think.

12. If you refuse to accept lies, you may end up empty-handed.

13. The status quo can be too progressive.

14. Ignorance has no cash value . . . unless you're a consultant.

15. If it's popular, claim credit. It it turns sour, attack it. Whatever you do, be sincere about it.

16. Never threaten anyone who roosts above you on the organizational chart.

17. Laughter has no accent.

18. Never be fooled by reality.

19. A pro bono a day keeps the lawyer away.

20. Checks are the DNA of politics.

21. If you want to control the outcome of a meeting, don't preside. Write the minutes.

22. When the wheels of Washington won't turn on snake oil, transpalmed cash helps.

23. If your position on an issue proves to be wrong, don't change your position; redefine the issue.

24. If you study a problem long enough, it may go away.

25. In politics, the frequent flush of money keeps the sewers of communications open.

26. Instead of more voice-activated recorders, the world needs more mind-activated voices.

27. For some politicians, graft is the minimum wage.

28. Never argue with a judge who is intestinally enriched.

29. A politician's handshake may be the foreplay to taxual assault.

30. POTOMALE: A di$h of political cornpone developed in the Valley of the Potomac; a mixture of fiscal mush generously laced with expensive pork, wrapped in corn shucks, and served with vote-getting brayalities.

31. The poor share; the rich grab. The needy serve; the greedy rule.

32. Taxes are for poor people; justice is for the rich.

33. The higher the perch, the shakier the ladder.

34. Never judge a mumble by its length but by its quality.

35. Former friends who revel may reveal.

36. Gotchadata: publishable but yet unpublished data or photographs which may be used for motivational purposes.

37. A well-fed cat won't eat your canary, and a well-greased palm won't slap a lobbyist.

38. Reincarnation offers no hope for Congressional reform.

39. Diogenes died in Washington . . . of exhaustion.

40. A palmiatrist is a specialist who trims calluses from the palms of politicians.

41. Loopholes are the rat holes of powerful PACrats.

42. Divorce lawyers specialize in bankruptcy.

43. Inaccurate mumbling can undermine a career.

44. Never abandon cash until you find something better.

45. Politicians may have an occasional affair with honesty, but they marry power.

46. Political feedback may turn out to be backupuncture.

47. Integrity in politics runs on batteries.

48. Cash is the balm for itchy palms.

49. Rumperatory abandon describes how some politicians walk and others think.

50. The quip tease of hate radio hosts is best measured by the burps and whines of their minds.

51. You may ignore facts, but never ignore people.

52. If the game of politics is based on wit, the final whistle blows at half time.

53. By definition, there is no celibate politician.

54. All that's stupid does not fail. The history of legislation proves it.

55. The most dangerous enemies are those you don't know.

56. In politics, nuggets of gold are outweighed by the slag of ignorance.

57. Boren Dictum: If you're going to be a phoney, be sincere about it.

58. Anger passes, but hatred lingers.

59. Numbers sprinkled into speeches give credibility to nonsense.

60. Never trust a court-appointed lawyer who advises the innocent to plea-bargain in order to avoid the risk of injustice in the court room.

61. Most lawyers worship the God of Billable Hours.

62. Be careful about studying the stupidity of your opponent; it may be contagious.

63. The nation needs fewer special prosecutors and more truth serum.

64. There are no plowshares in Washington.

65. Graft determines the draft of the Ship of State.

66. In politics, transpalmed cash is the essence of a meaningful handshake.

67. Naming the FBI building the J. Edgar Hoover Building is a continuing monument to the ethical standards of the Congress.

68. The Halls of Congress are filled with kitty litter... as the Congressional contribution to a clean environment.

69. For both Democrats and Republicans, the party line is at the bank.

70. Politicians rarely have sex with one another. What they do, they do to the public.

71. Bureaucrats make poor lovers, because they want to make feasibility studies at every step.

72. In politics, the power to subpoena is equivalent to a Colt .45.

73. Innovation is acceptable as long as it is within established guidelines.

74. People think; cash talks.

75. A lawyer's doodles on a yellow pad are a code for billable hours.

76. Hope springs eternal, but sleaze oozes.

77. Hype, punditry, and triviality are the media's trinity of political diversion.

78. Support the Clean Water Act. Never invite a politician into your hot tub.

79. Politician's Pledge of Allegiance: I pledge allegiance to the cash of the political action committees and for the favors for which it pays, one loophole, un-vetoable, with privileges not open to all.

80. Sniveling politicians suffer from an illness spread by excessive whining.

81. Not all fruitcakes are in bakeries.

82. The sacred robes of politicians are pants with big pockets.

83. Members of Congress should receive tax-free bonuses for each month they are out of session.

84. You can't fight when you're laughing.

85. The highest reality of politics is based on the lowest common denominator of people.

86. You can best learn about the pitfalls of life from the pratfalls of experience.

87. You can lead a politician to a committee meeting, but you can't make one think.

88. The present is the past of the future. Such profound thinking can make a politician the leader of a nation, or at least a Vice President.

89. The dancing shadows of candlelight may lead to romance but not to good government.

90. Spending your life making money costs too much.

91. Politicians often take umbrage, but they prefer cash.

92. The road to failure is often cluttered with little successes.

93. Agreeing with something in principle is a hedge against having to do anything about it.

94. In politics, brevity is the soul of obscurity.

95. An informed audience may become disruptive; fuzzify your speeches.

96. A cautious mouth gathers no foot.

97. If you're caught with your hand in the cookie jar, return the jar.

98. Some politicians are baptized by sprinkling bourbon, others by total immersion in cash.

99. Retreat gracefully . . . while looking for an opening.

100. Covet your neighbor's ignorance enough and it may become yours.

101. A reflective politician can turn his best profile at the flash of a camera.

102. Don't spend your time thinking about when, where, and how you will die; there's no future in it.

103. In politics, cleanliness is next to impossible.

104. The lawyer gives his client a book on near-death experiences to prepare him for the verdict.

105. Downloading ignorance on your computer is dumb.

106. Solemnity is used to cover ignorance.

107. Apathy is the condom that protects politicians from the people.

108. In early Spring, worms should sleep late.

109. We spend $450 billion to protect our shores from foreign enemies but we won't spend <u>one</u> billion for publicly financed campaigns to protect our system of government from special interests. We keep our national priorities straight: dirt is more important than people.

110. Beware of environmentalists who wish to build a monument to you; they may place it in a dog pound.

111. Politics is a fever in the head and an itch in the palm.

112. Forget Wall Street; invest in Senators.

113. Stupidity wrapped in the flag will prevail over wisdom wrapped in the law.

114. Most Members of Congress fear reincarnation because they may return on the wrong committee.

115. When poultry lobbyists roost with chickenhearted politicians, they share a nest of cash.

116. Beware of the politician who is sober-minded when he is drunk.

117. In a hot debate, don't use a single-shot musket in a high-tech war.

118. Too much lust can dim the luster of a career.

119. Beware of politicians whose eyes dilate when their palms open.

120. In Washington, most indecent proposals are written by lobbyists.

121. Talk about sex and people will forget about thievery.

122. Don't go before a tax judge who sings his decision; it's usually rap music for a bum rap.

123. Graduating from law school on a plea bargain opens the door for a successful political career.

124. If you lose track of the truth, be a person of your most recent word.

125. Arrogantual politicians treat their staff members like cats marking their territory.

126. Choose your battles carefully, and become the champion of the inevitable.

127. Over-reaction is a basic law of politics.

128. If you give a politician a free hand, he'll pick your pocket.

129. It is the job of the President and the Secretary of State to explain the foreign policy decisions made by the Pentagon and the defense contractors.

130. Proctologists are among the finest brain surgeons in Washington.

131. Selling Presidents and Members of Congress on the auction block is the foundation of our political free enterprise system.

132. In politics, ZIP does not refer to speed or energy. When you hear it, cross your legs, and keep your back to the wall.

133. Think tanks leak more than they think. Most are rusty.

134. Shallow thinking can lead to deep doodoo.

135. If you envy politicians, you don't understand politics.

136. Never stretch the truth more than is needed to cover your sleaze; some stretch should be held in reserve.

137. The rear view mirror approach to the future is OK if you can give it a new twist.

138. If you need meaningful advice, don't ask a toady.

139. The weak who care can conquer the strong who don't.

140. Capitol Hill is becoming known as Mortuary Hill where the truth is buried, and there is no prophecy of resurrection.

141. In politics, the jerks get the perks, the workers get the works, and the taxpayers get the bill.

142. Party platforms are written by fortune tellers shooting craps with alphabet soup.

143. The religious right moneyvangelists fulfill the profitsy of transpalmed cash.

144. Unfunded political mandate: term limits . . . without parole.

145. Born-again politicians are those who have just won reelection.

146. In the search for justice, clients with money go to trial; pro bonos go to settlement.

147. The toilets of Washington would be clogged if the members did not send newsletters to constituents.

148. Patriotic flag-waving can establish the porkal imperative of national security.

149. Praise your enemies so they may choke on your kindness.

150. If you can't lead, they won't follow.

151. Nothing is impossible until it is sent to a committee.

152. Happy are the accountants for they know the score.

153. You won't get lost if you stay in a rut.

154. If you keep your feet on the ground, you won't have far to fall.

155. When political magicians plant the flag in a barrel of pork, they have more up their sleeves than patriotism.

156. A New Year's Resolution for politicians is to diet by pigging out on a barrel of pork.

157. Politicians love the warm embrace of irrelevancy.

158. A regulation of a thousand words begins with a single sigh.

159. Never tell people more than you know.

160. Where there's a lie, there's a liar.

161. Lobbyists are taxidermists who stuff pockets with cash.

162. When an artist paints the portrait of a politician who has his hands in his own pockets, "the tubes will be twisted and dried".

163. Lawyers and justice rarely shake hands in a court of law.

164. The AQ (Assicity Quotient) is the relative measurement of a person's thinking or performance.

165. A moderate is one who is looking for a safe place to land.

166. Trashify your reports with irrelevant data, maps, footnotes, charts and graphs.

167. The Tooth Fairy is the official airline of sincere phonies.

168. The Boren Guidelines for Success: When in charge, ponder. When in trouble, delegate. When in doubt, mumble.

169. Preach the gospel of privatization and gather a few pieces of silver from above.

170. When necessary, truth can be the brush that cleans the political toilet. It is rarely used, unpleasant to reveal, but necessary to preserve everything but a career.

171. When you begin to believe what you are saying, it's time to give it some thought.

172. When the ice melts in a politician's drink, his speech loses its tinkle.

173. People who admire you for being an old politician may be confusing your political skills with fiber.

174. The ownership of television, radio and newspapers by a few corporations controls what, when, and how people think. It is called "the liberal media."

175. A politician's security blanket is national security.

176. An exit may be an outcome.

177. Don't spend all your ideas at once; save the other one for next year.

178. A stall should be converted into a prudent delay.

179. To prepare for politics, don't study the law; study lawyers.

180. Share confidences on your virtuous activities, but keep your vices to yourself. Today's friend may be tomorrow's enemy.

181. Today's politicians retire from office only when arthritis prevents them from opening their palms.

182. Loopholes constitute the fabric of the law.

183. Principle has nothing to do with politics, but principal does.

184. The nearest thing to honest graft is playing poker with a lobbyist.

185. An ignored lobbyist can be dangerous to your political health.

186. The politicians of the Christian Coalition will sometimes give up bribery for Lent.

187. Justice and injustice never balance on the fulcrum of politics.

188. The Republican Party has become the church of the Christian Coalition.

189. Political leadership is based on the roar, not the message; the studies, not the conclusions; the procedures, not the results; and the image, not the reality.

190. If you can't beat them, don't just join them; lead them.

191. Pomposity is the seat of political power.

192. Politicians and bureaucrats are the only people in the world who can say absolutely nothing and mean it.

193. When the three-dollar bill is established, the politicians will design it; the bureaucrats will spend it; and the taxpayers will pay the tab.

194. The ideas of many poliltians prove to be half-fertile at conception and half-baked at delivery.

195. Taxpayers who are sick and tired of politicians may have swallowed too many campaign promises.

196. If you want to have a favorable place in history, hire your own biographer.

197. If God hadn't meant for us to go to war, He wouldn't have given us guns.

198. The new wailing wall is the West Wall of the IRS Building.

199. When under attack, Republicans order more missiles; the Democrats plead not guilty.

200. The bipartisan duet has been postponed. The violinist lost his bow and the other lost his mind.

201. Some politicians get 28 promises per belch of gas.

202. Politicians like 'round the world junkets because the natives at home are restless.

203. Politicians with bar codes on their sleeves help lobbyists do their shopping.

204. Peace endangers national security.

205. In politics, the people around the country are not as important as the money under the table.

206. Experience does not assure wisdom.

207. Being stupid may not be optional but being ignorant is.

208. Ignorance is a basic Constitutional right.

209. Republicans are trying to invent the wheel, and Democrats are trying to decide what to do with it. Independents hold the axle.

210. Most politicians are fluent in English and BS . . . and English is their second language.

211. In the land of public apathy, corporations and the military can kill democracy—in the name of national security. And will.

212. Hypocrisy has no place in politics. It's everywhere.

213. Finding a genuine draft movement in politics is like finding a virgin in a house of ill repute.

214. Global corporations will make nations irrelevant. Incorporate and go on the Internet.

215. Politicians are less interested in interest rates than in well-heeled interest groups. Their music is political rock 'n roll.

216. The political theory of relativity relates the ratio of power and greed to weakness and apathy.

217. Never go to bed with a whistleblower.

218. Some people get ahead by plodding, others by plotting. The plod-plot axis tilts in favor of the plotters, and the plodders get the shaft.

219. Finding four honest politicians is like finding four aces, but don't bet on them. You can still be royally flushed.

220. Injustice seems to assert squatters' rights in some courtrooms.

221. Negative politicians are positive vote-getters, because voters know what they are against more than what they are for.

222. Being ethically disadvantaged is no disadvantage in politics.

223. Tax laws are for lawyers; tax decisions are for CPAs; tax burdens are for taxpayers.

224. Cinching the beltway around Washington merely concentrates the banditry.

225. The bottoms of conference tables are being refinished. Too many splinters.

226. Prioritize your conflicting loyalties before taking cash.

227. Old politicians never lie; they just fuzzify.

228. In Washington, the ethics committee is not permitted to enter the front door until the crooks have climbed out the alley window.

229. The function of a committee is to divide a problem into its constituent elements, and then nurture each element until it becomes a full-fledged problem itself.

230. Law without justice is like constipation without relief; it can lead to the death of the body politic.

231. Some politicians were not honest before they were elected.

232. More women must shake off their apathy or they will not be able to shake off their economic shackles—equal work for crapacious pay.

233. In politics, the louder the voice, the weaker the spine.

234. Though the Christian Coalition is the religion of the Republican Party, many Republicans want to return to honest conservatism.

235. Hate radio is part of the family values embraced by many idiotoxic politicians. They prey at the altar of greedocracy.

236. Politicians fear passing taxes, having to eat their own words, being laughed at, and being caught on tape.

237. Keep a pretty bulletin board and your mailing list up to date.

238. Learn from your mistakes and become recognized as a highly educated person.

239. Care enough to vote for the best or to buy the meanest.

240. Beware of carpetbaggers who know more about your state than you do.

241. Never take cash in front of a witness or a mirror.

242. Politicians exhort; crooks extort; and vice versa.

243. Always wear a shirt so you won't be identified by the hair on your chest.

244. Beware of the politician who lies with an accent . . . utterably untruthful.

245. When you see a politician, a lobbyist, and a lawyer conferring, be reverent. They may be the three wise men of I-Deal-ism.

246. Some judges deal justice from the bottom of the deck.

247. Divinity in politics is keeping a secret.

248. Do not confuse passion with compassion and do not become emotionally involved with a stranger.

249. Viagrafied cash is impregnating the body politic.

250. Politicians who have their hands out for lettuce should be given prunes.

251. In the dining room of politics, the menu may include armadillo on the half-shell, pickled chickens' feet, and toad dip & chips—any of which may be better than legislation on the half-bake.

252. Practice your speeches in private until you can recite them without laughing.

253. Ignorance and stupidity are but little potholes on the road to public office.

254. In politics, happy memories are often the product of bad memories.

255. An experienced bureaucrat is one who has done nothing before.

256. Money, like a squeaky bed, breeds jealousy.

257. Politicians believe that a half-truth plus a half-truth equals a whole truth, but the people wonder which half they are being given.

258. A filibuster is a marathon mumble . . . a gutsy sound of gusty substance.

259. The Information Age is more elderly than informative and more political than honest.

260. The information superhighway is numbered only by Swiss bank accounts.

261. Promises fade but handshakes are remembered... particularly those with transpalmed cash.

262. Noah's Ark once foundered on Mount Hokum where it was boarded by a horde of amorous politicians.

263. A politician who lies will steal.

264. You'll know you're a success if you can laugh all the way to the bank to borrow more money.

265. All candidates want change until they win.

266. Not many politicians are bilingual but most are bifacial.

267. If you think people doubt your patriotism, wear a little flag in your lapel.

268. Avoid excessive pomposity; stay out of rooms filled with politicians.

269. It is better to make yourself the butt of a joke than to stop short.

270. Too much of a good thing may be bad for your career, but feel free to be honest once a day.

271. You can't buy laughter but you can pay the price for not having it.

272. As a politician, you should realize that surviving a mid-life crisis can be worse than losing a post-life crisis. At least, you won't have to worry about counting the votes.

273. Politicians and television pundits who call vicious murder "ethnic cleansing" should have their mouths washed out with soap and their brains scoured with Brillo. This is linguistic cleansing.

274. God's greatest laughter may be at the seriousness with which pompous politicians take themselves.

275. You must believe that a free market and the equality of economic opportunity exist—as you ride on the back of the Tooth Fairy.

276. Hypocrisy has no place in politics. It's every-where.

277. Change the rules to meet each crisis and you can become known as a problem-solver even if you're solving the wrong problems.

278. The next revolution in America will come from the amalgam of money, weapons and public apathy—when democracy will be killed in the name of national security.

PART TWO.

Aptitudes, Talents,
and Strategies for Success

THE BOREN DICTUM

If you're going to be a phoney, be sincere about it.

There are many phonies in the world, but most of them do not know they are phonies. Not knowing their status, they bumble along with such unprofessional exhibitions of phoniness that they never bubble to the upper crust of the cesspool. There are phonies who sing joyous arias with great flamboyance, wild gestures, and vibrant warbles, but their blatancy can send chills down the spines of their targets. There are others who quietly, but just as joyously, hum the tunes of bureaucratic nonchalance, but the quietness of the humming makes them more difficult to detect. There are phonies in the political arena who know they are phonies but have practiced the art so long it is a natural expression of their being.

The saddest of all phonies are those who are genuine phonies, but don't know it. They hover around the founts of power; they are harsh as they echo the various pronouncements of their superiors; and they are overdropping as they name-drop in the games of politics.

As you move forward (sic) in your career, evaluate your political and bureaucratic skills. If you are a phoney, you must learn to be sincere about it. Sincerity is a vital enrichment factor. It includes the art of projecting heartfelt dedication, steadfast irrelevancy, constancy of purpose, and sensitivity of the soul. Sincere phonies are rarely suspected and always believed. If you are ready to make the personal commitment to follow this path, study the lessons of those who have gone before you.

First, to master the skills of the sincere phoney, you must establish a schedule for daily practice. Second, you must find a practice room where you can learn the expressive skills without possible embarrassment among friends or members of your family. You will need to experiment with different styles of body language and tonal patterns, and you must discover the ones with which you are the most comfortable.

You need not have much room, but you absolutely must have a mirror. A bathroom may be your best place to develop your skills. It usually has a mirror for practicing facial expressions, adequate room for arm-waving, and walls that can serve as an echo chamber as you develop your vocal expressions. Bathroom privacy is usually easy to achieve. If you need an extended period for practice, you can buy more time by occasionally spraying an air freshener through the keyhole or the bottom of the door. If you are a sensitive learner or have inquisitive people in your home, use a radio for enough background music to cover some of your vocalizations. Be creative and adventurous in your practice sessions.

Learn to assume various postures with which you can be comfortable. Try lifting your nose until the bridge is approximately parallel to the floor. Try a quiet sniff while paralleling your nose bridge and narrowing your eyes. If you have trouble with this exercise, buy a small package of limburger cheese or other appropriate stimulant. It may help you assume the proper air. After you are comfortable with these exercises, you may wish to add a second mirror to your practice sessions. It should be large enough for you to check your profile but not so large that it restricts your working space. A medium size hand mirror is adequate.

Begin to add to your practice sessions various exercises that concentrate on facial expressions. Furrow your brow, raise your eyebrows, squint one eye and then the

other eye. Simultaneous eye squints are not recommend-
ed. Alternately open, close, squiggle, rabbitize, and purse
your lips. Contract and flare the nostrils. Puff your
cheeks simultaneously, then alternately. Learn to p-popp
by relaxing your cheeks and your lips as you expel little
puffs of air. This exercise will help you when you are
ready to add neutral tones to your expressions.

After you have developed a nice inventory of facial
expressions, try a few head cockeries. Cock your head to
the right, then to the left. Raise your chin, both of them if
you have two. Practice mixing the cockeries with some of
the facial expressions.

After mastering the facial expressions and the head
cockeries, add a few hand gestures, shoulder shrugs, and
slow or vigorous arm movements. It is vital to develop
some expressive hand gestures. Do not point your finger
at anyone before you unless you wish to express anger.
For most purposes, if you must use a finger gesture, point
upward or downward. It is far better to use open-palm
hand gestures, since they do not transmit a threat. The
open palm should be in a vertical position and accompa-
nied by a slow and "soft" movement. If you want to use a
palm-up hand gesture, use both palms and use them in a
supplicational manner. If you are a politician, you may
use the open-palm upward gesture, because it can express
friendliness as well as an unspoken invitation to a cashistic
transpalmation.

After mastering the body language, introduce into
your practice session a few tonal patterns. Try varying the
octaves of single tones. Jump from one-level tones to
multiple tones. Combine tonalities for pleasing combina-
tions. Crisp staccato tones can be mixed with trombone-
like slurring, but each should be projected with utmost sin-

cerity. Try thrusting your chin forward, tilt your head
upward slightly, open your eyes very wide raise your eyebrows, lift both hands in a slow suplicating manner.

Daily mirror practice is imperative, and extra practice session during the day are bonuses you should seek
when possible. Some beginners practice while traveling to
work or while walking in shopping centers. Shop windows displaying dark items such as clothing, carpets or
drapes are excellent for quick-glance reflection purposes.
If you are driving to work, turn the rear view mirror so
you can see yourself. Try mixing mumbling with the various gestures. Remember, however, you should: (1) keep
one hand on the steering wheel and one eye on the road,
and (2) stop practicing when you approach a stop light.
The driver in the car next to you may report you to the
police or a nearby institution.

After you have mastered these basics, you can turn
to the most important of them all: the skill of maximizing
the pupillary contact. That is, you should stare intently in
the pupil of one eye of your target person. You can develop
this skill to a limited extent in your practice room by staring into the mirrored image of your own eye. Fix your
gaze on the pupil of one eye. If you shift your gaze from
one eye to the other, you will appear to be shifty. Pick one
eye and stick to it. There is no political implication in
choosing either the right or the left eye; select the one you
feel most comfortable with. Once you have made the pupillary contact maintain it regardless of outside influences.
Imitate the Palace Guards in London. As you approach
what you feel to be the climax, mask the face with as serious an expression as you can muster. As you continue your
mumble, raise your eyebrows, and use slow and graceful
movement of the hands to accentuate the sincerity factor

as well as to supplicate somewhat prayerfully. Tilt your head slightly forward and perhaps slightly to the right or left, furrow your brow, then slowly nod your head up and down. This is the invitation. When your target returns the head nod, you have it made. There has been no communication - no transfer of information - but your target has agreed with whatever you have not said.

As soon as you have the concurring nod, extricate yourself from the situation. Do it with a warm smile and a hand-on-hand handshake. Express gratitude or joy through a brief smile. Then leave immediately. Leave before the ethereal spirit of the phonistic trance is lost. Do not break the pupillary contact until you turn your head in departure. Don't run, but move out as rapidly as dignity will permit.

If you wish to try the graduate level, you can use your phonification skills in a group situation. The same instructions apply, except you must maximize the pupillary contact with one person until he or she nods and looks away. Make other contactual sweeps of the room until you have a number of turnheads nodding with you. Reinforce the concurring nods by returning to each head-nodder for a seconding nod. You will learn that the second, return-nod is almost immediate. If you find a negative person in the group, concentrate on that person, and implement an extended pupillary contact. After the negative one turns his or her head, continue pupillarizing until the target gives you a second glance. At that time, give a slight nod to confirm your victory. In my many years of experience on the speaking circuit, I have never encountered a negative person whom I could not neutralize by extended pupillary contact.

Success as a sincere phoney is built victory upon victory and phoniness upon phoniness. When you have mastered the art, stride forth into any arena with the confident air of one who has the world by the tail. To thine own self be sincere.

APTITUDES

From amongst the mountains, the valleys, the plains, the islands of the seas, and the classrooms of the schools, young men and women are considering a career in politics. They have read the words of the prophets; they have pondered the thoughts of the philosophers; and they have studied the records of office-holders whose public service was filled with such values as honesty, truth, and integrity. Public service was then of the OLD DEMOCRACY, when people knew and cared about their government . . . and honesty was more than a curious concept.

Now it has come to pass that a NEW DEMOCRACY has evolved from another set of values . . . values which stress servicing the people rather than serving them. Since many of the young men and women who are now prodigiously pondering a political career have no experience in working on or around a farm, they do not know the difference between servicing* and serving. They are therefore, at a serious disadvantage as they seek to assess their values, their aptitudes and their readiness for a political career. The JB-PAT (Jim Boren Political Aptitude Test) was born to assist political aspirants in making such an evaluation. The test will reveal to them the level of their acceptance of greedery, sleezality, and two-facedness. There are no right or wrong answers to the questions of

---

*A bull services a cow; a true public servant serves the people.

the test. The scores merely permit a person to compare his or her interests, abilities and potential with others who may explore the same political careers. No wise person, however, should enter politics without the evaluative assistance of JB-PAT, the first aptitude test to be in harmony with the new greedocratic philosophies of gititwhilethegittinsgood and tahellwitheverbodyells.

The Jim Boren Political Aptitude Test (JB-PAT)

If you are thinking of a career as a politician, the JB-PAT may help you make an informed decision about your potential for success. The test is designed to help you evaluate your values as well as your readiness to develop the skills that are common to most of today's successful politicians. The validity of the test will depend upon the temporary honesty with which you answer the questions. If you enjoy being sleazy and two-faced in your dealings with other people, the test will be of little help to you if you answer the questions as you think some honest do-gooder would answer them. Answer all the questions even if you don't know what they mean.

JB-PAT TEST

Directions: On a scale of 0 to 5, you should circle the number that more or less reflects your views or abilities. If you totally disagree, circle the "0"; if you completely agree, circle the "5". Though it may be appropriate, do not circle all five numbers.

012345 When I see money, my palms itch.

012345 I can look people in the eye while lying.

012345 When I do nothing, I can do it with style.

012345 I can control my lust in public.

012345 I can kiss babies when their swaddling clothes are wet but, in public, I do not kiss babies past puberty.

012345 I find joy riding in parades when I am in the first vehicle.

012345 I know the words to the first stanza of the Star Spangled Banner.

012345 My bladder is large and controllable.

012345 I can wave the national flag with great energy, sustained enthusiasm and appropriate patriotism.

012345 I can smoke without inhaling; I can drink without swallowing; I can lie without moving my lips.

012345 Without detection, I can palm cash following a meaningful handshake.

012345 I can talk baseball, football, basketball, Baptist, Methodist, Catholic, stock market, and other religions.

012345 I can laugh at jokes with no punch lines as well as jokes I do not understand.

012345 When I make promises, I keep no notes.

012345 When I am a phoney, I am sincere about it.

012345 I have memorized the names of several famous poets, authors, philosophers, and rock musicians.

012345 I can stay awake in boring meetings.

012345 My conscience and my memory are convenient to me.

012345 (For men) I have had a vasectomy. (For women) I have had my tubes tied.

012345 I can quote several multi-purpose verses from the Bible.

012345 I can appear to be attentive while listening to dumb ideas from stupid people who are contributors.

012345 I can stand, talk, and smile during parties even though my feet and my back hurt.

012345 I know when is is is and when is is was, and I know how to be sincere when I mislead under oath.

Jim Boren's Political Aptitude Test (JB-PAT) (Continued)

Directions: Circle the letter of the answer which you think to be best.

1. Husbands and wives of politicians should be:
    a. friendly smilers, poised backdrops, and loyal toadies who can fawn and grovel with dignity.
    b. absolutely brilliant, articulate in expression, and well-informed on the issues.
    c. able to accept insults without appearing to recognize them.

2. Candidates should use flashy television spots with stirring music and minimal substance, because:
    a. they capture the attention of intelligent voters.
    b. voters with short attention spans prefer to see, hear and emote rather than think.
    c. they inspire people to think about the principles enunciated by the nation's founding fathers.

3. Today's successful politicians are those who:
    a. appear to be sincere as they solemnly swear on the Bible.
    b. always tell the truth.
    c. will not lie to win the support of people who have more money than brains.

4. Political barbecues are useful campaign occasions for politicians who can:
    a. explain the American system of checks and balances.
    b. swallow cold, dry, greasy meat while smiling and nodding to the sponsoring committee.
    c. deliver a meaningful and long oration on a major campaign issue.

5. Effective political speeches are those which:
    a. inform the voters on significant issues.
    b. stir the crowd to support campaign reform.
    c. identify the candidate's prejudices with the prejudices of the audience.

6. In most campaigns, honesty is so rare that candidates should:
    a. forget it, and get on with whatever will win votes.
    b. identify and nurture any shred of truth that may be found.
    c. find a peaceful retreat where they can study the ideas of
       Plato, Voltaire, and Al Capone.

7. Assume you are part of the power structure of a state . . . Texas,
   for example. If you know you are losing the race as the polls
   close on Saturday, the election day, you should:
    a. steal all the unmarked cash you can find, then catch a
       plane to Rio de Janeiro.
    b. stop counting all ballots at midnight Saturday, so you can
       steal whatever number of votes you need in order to win
       the governorship when the counting resumes next week.
       (Check Texas, 1956)
    c. draft an inspiring concession speech that will renew the
       peoples' faith in the orderly processes of our government.

PART ONE: Total the values of all circled numbers. (The highest
possible score is 115. 5 x 23 = 115) If your score is 115, thy success
as a politician is assured. If your score is 105, you can achieve moderate success in politics. If your score is 90, you should not consider
becoming a candidate, but you should consider entering a related field
. . . such as the law, moneyvangelism, or special interest lobbying. If
your score is less than 80, find some honest work.

PART TWO: The best answers for successful political practitioners
are: 1-a, 2-b, 3-a, 4-b, 5-c, 6-a, 7-b. For success in politics or the
related fields, you should have a perfect score in Part Two.

BASIC SKILLS

When in charge, ponder.

When in trouble, delegate.

When in doubt, mumble.

When in Charge, Ponder.

Dynamic inaction, doing nothing but doing it with style, is one of the most important concepts that can undergird a successful career for any bureaucrat or politician. By doing something, one can make a mistake, but doing nothing but doing it with style can give one all the advantages of having done something without the accompanying risk of making a mistake. The image of performance, therefore, is safer than performance itself. One of

55

the most effective ways of projecting the image of performance through dynamic inaction is through prodigious pondering.

Many people have the ridiculous idea that when they are in charge of some program, event, or organization, they are supposed to do something. They feel an obligation to exert some leadership, to direct, to manage, to show results. Such people, whether they know it or not, are on a short-term career track. They may zoom across a bureaucratic landscape or a political moonscape with great vim and vigor, but they will find that the field is not level. It will be tilted against them, and the tilt may not be evident until it is too late to salvage a career.

Other people may flash across the corporate skies with the brilliance and fire of a meteor, but they will burn out or find their career headed for an irreversible crash. Beginning administrators in academe may make far-reaching plans for new approaches to education, and they may prudently clear all of their plans with the governing board of the institution. When one of these administrators seeks to put the plan into effect by a sudden and non-participatory approach to a faculty, the leadership will be converted into a pleadership. Beginners sometimes confuse <u>positions</u> of leadership with <u>needs</u> for actual leadership, and this can result in an abstructional impediment to a career.

The wise old bureaucrats or battle-scarred politicians who are in charge of some program or organization know that the strategy of prodigious pondering is an effective and successful one to follow. They know they can convey the image of leadership and express deep concern without making a commitment. A well-executed ponder is a marvel to observe.

To project an image of deep thought and concern,

the successful manager must develop a number of techniques in non-committal communication - a vital element in implementing a philosophical modality of dynamic inaction. Most important of these are a series of facial expressions. Their mastery requires private practice before a mirror.

Assume, for example, a proposal has been made in a board meeting or public session of aroused citizens. The beginner might mistakenly flutter with a quick and logical response. The experienced ponderer, on the other hand, will purse the lips, squint one eye, tilt the head upward, and gaze intently at the corner of the room where the walls meet the ceiling. A slight, vertical nod and a stroke of one chin may indicate a process of profound thinking. A prolonged ponder may be puctuated by a mumbled tonality or an assessing grunt. The prolonged ponder can be followed by a slow visual sweep of the members of the audience. If someone seems inclined to say something, the ponderer can raise an eyebrow and slowly nod as one hand is lifted with an outward palm, fingers upward. The outward palm-lift will indicate that it is not the time for audience participation. Audience participation must never interrupt a ponderer's ponder because pondering is never an effective weapon in confrontation.

Pondering is a vital skill for public office holders and corporate executives. When one is confronted by an angry voter or stockholder, a well-executed ponder can be the most appropriate extractionary move. When a spouse asks a question which the ponderer wishes to avoid, does not hear, or does not understand, a short-term ponder may provide noncommunicative escape. Cocktail parties and formal receptions are excellent places for little ponders. The tinkling of ice in a glass, the crunchy sounds of celery, the sizzling of chicken-livers-wrapped-in-bacon-and-speared-with-cellophaned-toothpicks, the mumbles of the crowd, and other sounds may make the sparkling inanities of conversation difficult to hear. A smile, a lifted brow, and a nondirective mumble can complement the facial gestures of a ponder and add class to the encounter.

Both beginning and experienced ponderers should practice the styles they find personally to be most comfortable and effective. Little ponders, big ponders, free-style ponders and prolonged ponders can become part of the inventory of ponders which can add to the confidence and the success of any bureaucrat or politician. A ponder, like a mumble, can never be quoted.

Ponderer's Practice Sheet

By daily practice before a mirror or at a desk, you can perfect and retain a wide range of skills as a prodigious ponderer. You must project total sincerity and sympathetic authority. Feel free to add to this list or adjust any technique to whatever style is most comfortable for you. Read Chapter 5: The Boren Dictum on the mastery of being a sincere phoney.

1. With brow lifted, eyes downward, mouth tightly closed inwardly, slowly straighten a paper clip . . . or bend it into different shapes.
2. Hands clasped behind your head, place your lower lip over your upper lip; gaze upward.
3. With your mouth closed, expand each cheek simultaneously or alternately with intermittent pops of air.
4. With one thumb based at your temple, rub your brow with one to four fingers.

5. Stroke your throat with a thumb on one side, forefinger on the other.

6. Head downward, lightly hold the top of your head with thumb and index fingers (similar to grasping a ripe cantaloupe), lightly massage your scalp.

7. Lips pursed; left arm folded across your chest; other elbow in hand; thumb under chin; gaze at light fixture.

8. If you have a swivel chair, swivel back and forth in a thirty degree arc, or gaze out a window.

9. Thumb at base of cheek, hand over mouth, eyes upward or downward.

10. If at a desk, place chin in one hand, tap fingers of other hand on desk. Simultaneously or sequentially. If not at a desk, scratch the lobe of your left ear with your right hand.

11. Place upper lip over lower lip. Stare vacantly.

12. Gaze at the far corner of the room, squinting one eye.

13. Combine the whispered sounds of the letters "p" and "q" while drawing a boobidoodle on a note pad. Vary the frequency of the p-popping or q-quattles.

14. Flip one of your thumbs outwardly from your upper teeth. If you have an upper bridge, flip your upper lip.

15. Head upward, eyes downward, pull at the lobe of one ear.

16. With your eyes fixed on some nearby object, slowly scratch your head. End the scratch by running your hand over your head and massage your neck two or three times.

17. With thumb and second index finger, smooth your eye brows in an inward to outward stroke beginning at the bridge of your nose.

18. Pull up some report or old document on your computer. Gaze at the screen and purse your lips from time to

time. Keep a solemn countenance on your face.

19. With thumb on one cheek and fingers on the other, squeeze in about four times. The squeezing will let people know you are awake.

20. With your thumb on your jaw, stroke your first and second chin with your index fingers.

When in Trouble, Delegate.

When most newcomers to the world of politics and bureaucracy see trouble coming their way, they tend to duck, run, or hide. A few, however, foolishly may prepare to deal with the problem in a forthright manner. Those who take a direct path in dealing with troublesome problems will not survive to the age of retirement or attain the higher levels where the levers of power are polished. With directness, there is no flexibility of rumperatory movement ... no means of dispersing the impact of a problem when it clunkates with great force. The duckers, runners, and hiders may be survivors, but they will not survive with important images of dignity and class.

How can you achieve survival with dignity and class without necessarily knowing what you are doing? How can you pompistrut your way from the bull's-eye of problem impaction? What are the skills you must develop in order to thrive, not merely survive?

As you seek the answers to these questions, you will be developing your personal inventory of effective crisis-control techniques. You must develop those techniques with which you are the most comfortable. Like an old shoe that has stretched to match the operational contours of the delegator, the techniques may bear the scruff marks of a few close calls, but they are ready when the big tests come.

There are few things sadder than to witness a clumsy or awkward delegation. Enjoy the process, and learn as you go.

Residuation. At the first rumbling of a distant problem, residuate. That is, burrow into a fixed, immovable position, and maintain the lowest possible profile. People living in the region of Oklahoma known as Tornado Alley know the value of timely residuation. At the first hint of tornadic action, they quickly residuate. Whether it be in a roadside ditch, storm cellar, basement, or central room of a house, the residuators stay put until the storm has passed. Similarly, experienced politicians and bureaucrats know the value of residuating or squattling their way through crises. At the first rumbling signal, don't hesitate; residuate! Residuation should be an immediate action. It is better to be an over-residuator than an under-residuator.

Hunkerfication. Residuation may not be practical in instances when the crisis situation may extend over a long period of time. Timality stretch may require hunkerfying. Whereas physical hunkering is to be "at the ready" or in a crouched position in such sports as football, grunt-and-groan wrestling, and back-alley crap games, political or bureaucratic hunkerfying is a mental or psychological crouch . . . a state of mental neutrality that is maintained until the hunkerfier can determine the drift of the crisis or its related issues. The hunkerfier can then leap into whatever position that will be best for his or her career. Hunkerfication, a step above residuation, is practiced not only in politics but also at senior management levels in religious, corporate and academic bureaucracies.

All successful politicians, even frightened ones, are effective hunkerfiers. They check the mood of voters and big-money givers until unrest among them builds to a dangerous level. They hunkerfy until they are ready to spring into a position of thundering leadership. Timing, rhetorical roaring, and polished pompistrutting help the hunkerfier move with certainty to the top.

Academic bureaucrats, members of the clergy, and football coaches tend to be in a state of constant hunkerfication. Every layperson believes he or she knows as much or more that these bureaucrats, and they can prove it with the analysis of questionable decisions, meddling sermons, or fourth-down-and-one end runs. This is one of the reasons that most university presidents, members of the clergy, and football coaches change jobs with great frequency.

Hall-searching. In some organizations, hall-searching can be used as an unofficial but effective type of direct delegation. That is, the delegator simply strolls the halls until an empty office is spotted, and the problem papers can be slipped from a file folder directly into the unattended in-box. Success in the maneuver requires deftness in the toss and rapidity in the retreat.

Decision Postponement and Committee Processes.

High level politicians and bureaucrats often use the "committee with ruffles" technique. They appoint a study committee, but they designate it as a "Blue Ribbon Commission" or a "Special Task Force." The titles elevate the status of the committees, and it indicates the delegator places great importance to the problem. The name of the committee is merely a part of the image game. Whatever it is called, a committee is a committee.

Decision postponement provides a simple and safe escape from fixed responsibility, but it does so within the apparent environment of prudent management. If a decision involves the expenditure of money, it should be referred to the comptroller, the treasurer, the administrative officer or any and all functionaries who may have a modicum of jurisdiction. Including them seems to be proper; it makes them happy; and it buys more time.

If the decision to be postponed involves a personnel matter, include the office of human resources in the process. Such functionaries will feel better about being

included, and their future friendship may be helpful to
you. More important, an extended delay may be effected.
Personnel or human resource specialists are usually
among the last to know about an organization's new policies or new operational directions. Playing "catch-up"
adds to institutional confusion and it provides businesslike
delay.

     If you need a short postponement, find some minor
question of policy or overlap to refer to the Office of the
General Counsel. This will provide a delay of at least six
months, and it helps in developing a favorable working
relationship with the lawyers. They may grumble about
their work load, but in reality, the lawyers respect people
who appear to respect them and their decisions. Lawyers
are like pieces of military artillery; it is better to have their
mouths aimed away from you than toward you. Cultivating
an organization's lawyers, therefore, may prove beneficial
to you in the future when you might be able to influence
the mouthal aim.

     When it is wise to have a long postponement,
return to the committee process. In their finest form, committees can embrace a single problem, carefully caress it
with loving words and happy mumbles, and then divide
the problem into its constituent parts. Each part is then
stroked and nurtured until it becomes a full-fledged problem itself. This division of problems contributes to the
growth of bureaucracy and it entangles the political
process. What an exciting concept! And what a marvelous technique to include in your political or bureaucratic arsenal of weapons. Decision postponement and interface avoidance can be orchestrated with artistry and style.
Practice this approach whenever you can. You need to
practice all aspects of this process so you will be prepared

for managing a crisis.

Nothing is impossible until it is sent to a committee.

When in Doubt, Mumble.

The origin of mumbling is one of the elusive mysteries of life. Scholars have long sought to unravel the mystery, because hidden within the threads of this ancient fabric may be the design for life itself - the design for joy and sadness, harmony and disruption, love and hate, peace and war. What, when, and where was the original mumble? What wisdom lay within the first resonating sound of subsagacious thought?

Was the first mumble the one of astonishment that rose from a single cellular "Wow!" at the sound of the Big Bang? Was it the hesitant acceptance of temptation by Adam and Eve in the Garden of Eden? Could it have been the exclamatory expression of discovery when the first finger was burned, or when the invention of the wheel gave birth to the first Welcome Wagon? Was it during the first session of solemn-faced lawyers as a member of their species attempted to define for them the meaning of "sex" within a non-sexual context? Was "is" is, or was "is" was? Could the first mumble have come as a distant echo from a meeting of stockholders, politicians, or preachers?

Whatever its origin, one fact is unquestioned. Mumbling, the great art of the unknowing expressing the unknown, or hiding the known is the prevailing communicative tool in today's bureaucracies. Its ancient threads provide the woof and warp of the fabrical institutions of the world. And when these institutions or its members are threatened, the mumble helps them survive.

Regardless of the language or the culture of a soci-

ety, research during my extensive travels throughout all the
states of my native land, as well as fifty-eight other
nations, reveals there are two basic approaches to mumbling: linear and vertical. Both have great value when
used separately, but the skillful blending of the two can lift
the mumbler to great heights of professionalism.

• Linear Mumbling •

Linear mumbling is the transposition of tonal patterns. It is not distinguishable in the form of words though
a few words may be used as linear connectors among the
mumbles. Flexible tones, octave changes, exhaliatory projections, orchestrated fade-out or diaphramic gruntations
can be connected or loosely linked by an occasional word
or two. "Thrummum tooble ummmmmphotah the interest
rates vicassitomble lottawattakatumka." When anyone
hears a linear mumbler practicing the art, the initial
response is to lean forward in an effort to catch some
meaning that might be embodied in the tonal pattern. The
significance of linear mumbling lies not in its meaning but
in its avoidal expression. The listener will usually respond
with a knowing nod of acceptance.

Linear mumblers smile, nod, shake hands, and
move on to the next smile, nod, shake, and mumble.

Politicians who think they recognize a contributor
but can't remember the name, corporate executives who
think they have spotted a major stockholder but are not
sure, and academic leaders who work the crowd at alumni
reunions can use linear mumbling as a means of extricat-
ing themselves from embarrassing situations. Each can
turn to his or her spouse, and linearize an introduction.
"Honey, you remember Dstsummbalmmmm, don't you?"

The experienced spouse will speak to the person being introduced, "I'm sorry. I didn't hear your name." At that point the ignorant mumbler tunes in to pick up the name as it is given to the spouse. Another smile, nod, shake and mumble.

Once when speaking to the annual banquet of the Fort Myers Chamber of Commerce, I linearized my way through the entire receiving line period. Standing by the wife of the Chamber president, I greeted each guest with an extended hand, a smile, eye contact, an affirmative head nod, and a mumble. "Hello, I'm Jim Boren. thrummum etch dooblatchal." Each guest smiled, shook, nodded, and moved on down the line. Not one person asked what I had said, but each seemed happy to have met the speaker.

Now, quatchumm attick dorumble-kkech as we learn to mumble vertically.

• Vertical Mumbling •

Vertical mumbling is characterized by stringing multisyllabic words that avoid simplicity and hide intent. The stringing of words may consist of short bursts of articulate multisyllabattics - the forceful or clunkal interfacing of words - or they may be composed of an extended flow of multisyllabic words. "Verticality of joyful mumblistics tend to supernalize the harmonic modalities of nondirective thought patterns and thereby project a vertical engoosation of idiotoxicities and marginal clunkations. And it should be done as soon as possible."

Vertical mumbling may be used to avoid confrontation, but it is usually used to indicate great expertise when none exists. As an avoidance language, a comprehensive vertical mumble may be elevated in its resonating tonalities to project a slight hint of concurrence before the mumble ends. In other words, the art of vertical mumbling can indicate full comprehension of the matter at issue, a complete grasp of all the variables involved, and a concurring professional bailout. As the language of the expert, it can also project an air of confidence and poise.

In perfecting your skill in vertical mumbling, try constructive emulation. Find some vertical mumbler for whom you have respect, and listen carefully to his or her flow of words. If you hear a few phrases that are eloquently evasive or marginally profound, make note of them. As you are driving your car or in the privacy of your bathroom, practice the words and phrases until they are a part of your vocabulary. Listen to the radio or watch the television news. The politicians or economic forecasters who are guests on Sunday morning punditry shows are excellent sources of vertical mumbles. The pundits themselves are outstanding harrrrumphals. If you are in desperate need of a quick tune-up before making a speech or presenting a report, check C-Span or tune in to some huckstering moneyvangelist.

During World War II, an officer in the Canadian Air Force developed a three-column system of wordational mumbling. On a speaking trip to Ottawa, I visited a friend who was the senior personnel official with the Ministry of Defense. We were able to locate the office where the three-column system originated, but no one could recall the name of the truly Great Communicator. On June 28, 1968, as the President of the International Association of Professional Bureaucrats, I presented the organization's first Distinguished Service Award to Phillip Broughton, an officer with the U. S. Public Health Service. He "rediscovered" the work of the Canadian officer. The discoverer and rediscoverer merit special tribute by all bureaucrats. The three-column fuzzword generator is an effective tool to help beginning mumblers perfect their use of the art form. I have developed many sets of the fuzzword generators, and am pleased to include several for the use of those who wish to become competent mumblers.

When in doubt, mumble

status quo

OOPS!

INATAPROBU*

*International Association of Professional Bureaucrats

FUZZWORD GENERATORS

Instructions: To construct political or bureaucratic fuzzifications (enhanced vertical mumbles), think of any three-digit number. Select a corresponding word from each column, left to right, and you will be able to speak with "mandated irrelevant committee". That is I - 626. The use of numbers is for the ease of primary learning, but they may be dropped as you master the technique. You may let your mumbles flow with joyful abandon as long as the flow is from left to right. Feel free to cross-fertilize the words moving among the different sets. Try it. "The I - 681 of the IRS may produce a II - 682 which can result in a I - 750." Or . . . "When the III - 603 is orbitated with IV - 1, V - 1, III - 3, you may as well as give up!"

Group I: Basic Political Mumbles

0 orchestrated	0 policy	0 asssessment
1 substantive	1 rhetorical	1 methodology
2 drivelated	2 irrelevant	2 sleaze
3 hype-oriented	3 mental-neutral	3 disinformation
4 jobs-related	4 proactive	4 infidelity
5 innovative	5 bailout	5 fauxtegrity
6 mandated	6 strategic	6 committee
7 cumulative	7 political	7 caucus
8 functional	8 cash-flow	8 Lewinsky factor

Group II: Administrative Judgements

0 Blackstonian	0 courtroom	0 precedents
1 Miranda's	1 howlistic	1 misapplication
2 annotated	2 procedural	2 judgement
3 coparcenated	3 abatable	3 corporate veil
4 acknowledged	4 contractual	4 covenant
5 fuzzified	5 bilateral	5 equity
6 collateralized	6 fiscality	6 cohabitation
7 gravementalized	7 procurement	7 tenancy
8 slushmentalized	8 grand jury	8 impleadership
9 God-fearing	9 spiritual	9 interface

Group III: Corporate Orbitations

0 incredimentalized	0 investment	0 portfolio
1 pragmatic	1 viable	1 adventure
2 tax-free	2 procurement	2 subsidiary
3 abstructed	3 technological	3 strategies
4 encumbered	4 liability	4 debenture
5 subordinated	5 infrastructural	5 feasibility
6 recapitalized	6 evidential	6 revenues
7 unitized	7 managerial	7 down-sizing
8 vested	8 vacuumental	8 precedent
9 preferred	9 inflationary	9 prime

Group IV: Congressional Idiotoxicities

0 comprehensive	0 multilateral	0 dialogues
1 documented	1 crisis-oriented	1 capability
2 adjustive	2 cash	2 graspalities
3 meaningful	3 retropuntal	3 handshake
4 amended	4 exclusionary	4 transpalmations
5 enriched	5 under-the-table	5 graft
6 untaxed	6 special interest	6 contributions
7 untraceable	7 compensatory	7 amendment
8 randomized	8 motivational	8 cloture
9 quantitative	9 conservative	9 summitry

Group V: Rhetorical Liquidity

0 moderated	0 anticipatory	0 criteria
1 unique	1 historo-cultural	1 capability
2 subsagacious	2 reversible	2 contrition
3 regressive	3 internettal	3 format
4 web-searched	4 multiphasic	4 resonance
5 prioritized	5 private sector	5 field audit
6 retrofitted	6 resource-intensive	6 modalities
7 thunderated	7 Congressional	7 fluctuations
8 open-palmed	8 empirical	8 pay-offs
9 drivelated	9 ya-know	9 dynamics

Group VI: For Use by Athletes and Sportscasters

0 ahhhh	0 ya-know	0 team spirit
1 anduhhhh	1 wellluh	1 great fans
2 yaknow itz great	2 annnnnah	2 a cracked rib
3 duhball	3 hittttem	3 hamstring
4 uhhh-huhh	4 wellahhhh	4 upforthagame
5 like-yaknow	5 yeahhhhh	5 concussion
6 yeah-yaknow-uhhhh	6 one-uhh-them	6 injuries
7 like-itzthisway	7 yaknow	7 stomppum
8 and-yaknow-itz-ahhh	8 exactly	8 gonnagettum

Group VII: Boren Chordations

0 bladderated	0 monomental	0 nincompoopery
1 supportable	1 tabulated	1 exfritterature
2 oopsified	2 anticipatory	2 intervoidance
3 reciprocated	3 pompitstrutting	3 dementia
4 vested	4 fiduciary	4 breakthrough
5 maximized	5 personpower	5 rationale
6 industrialized	6 cross-cultural	6 thruput
7 spiraling	7 recessionary	7 GNP
8 retroanalyzed	8 bottom-line	8 impaction

Mumblepower Test

Check your developing mumblepower: Borenwords for Career Enhancement

___1. hunkerfication
___2. globation
___3. idiotoxic
___4. fuzzifications
___5. residuation
___6. profundification
___7. zilchification
___8. boobilation
___9. invervoidal
___10. positosity
___11. exfritterature
___12. oopsification
___13. chazzipper
___14. Mount Hokum
___15. taxcoma
___16. cootle
___17. pappetry
___18. componement
___19. abstruction
___20. scurrency

a. a ministerial tonal pattern
b. maintaining a minimal profile
c. poisonously dangerous because of the idiocy on which it is based
d. postponing an issue by sending it to a committee
e. relaxation with a bundle of memorandum
f. deep and involved expression of something simple
g. porosity of logic; a position full of holes
h. something that is marginally sound converted into something that is unquestionably stupid
i. converting something of value into nothingness
j. a career-oriented psychological crouch
k. A Congressional chant
l. with built-in adjustivity of future interpretation
m. Washington's Capitol Hill/ Ottawa's Parliament Hill
n. an appropriation that is frittered away
o. confrontation avoidance
p. a state of being that results from heavy taxes
q. a chastity zipper for politicians (bipartisan)
r. fractured infrastructure
s. a minor error
t. computerized decision
u. money that scurries about the financial landscape in search of a value base
v. biggest of the Big Pictures
w. the filler of a puff piece
x. a chortle of an old coot
y. an implemented plopple
z. destruction of an idea or policy by making it so abstract that no one can understand it.
aa. a tax cut for the poor

Answers to the Mumblepower Test

1. j	7. i	13. q	19. z
2. v	8. h	14. m	20. u
3. c	9. o	15. p	
4. l	10. g	16. x	
5. b	11. n	17. w	
6. f	12. s	18. d or t	

Profundifying and Fuzzifying

Once you have mastered the basics of vertical and linear mumbling, you should practice mumbling until you can drivelate immediately and with style. Drivelating, the art of producing drivel with professional eloquence, is one of the skills of a long-term survivor in any organization. While drivelating may provide you with survival, it can carry you only so far up the ladder of success. To thrive and rise to the higher levels of success, you must learn to profundify and fuzzify.

The function of profundifying is to express a simple idea in profound terms. Profundified words and phrases may dance around an issue without disturbing the neutral thought patterns of bureaucrats, politicians or members of boards of directors. Analysis of a profundification, however, will reveal that there is an idea which underlies the words. Accomplished primarily through the use of Roget's Thesaurus, profundifying can lull a lazy listener or reader into a mental slumber while the profundifier can be accurate in his or her message without alarming the intended recipient. Since typical listeners or readers do not evaluate or judge the thrust of a statement, the profundifications are rarely challenged.

Nearly all presidents or prime ministers have been outstanding profundifiers, but even the best may occasionally fall below the professional level expected of such leaders. For example, in President Clinton's greatest crisis, he engaged in simple hair-splitting and low level mumbling as he explained his interpretation of non-participatory sex. He would have done better if he had profundified through using such phrases as "a recipiently oriented pattern of heterosexuality" . . . or "a personally shared concept as expressed through a singular but private articulation." This would have expressed the President's view that he received but did not necessarily participate in a reciprocal pattern of giving and taking.

A Texas lawyer and a CPA used a Borenword as they profundified an amended tax return they submitted to the Internal Revenue Service. One of their clients was in jail for accepting a $35,000 kickback. The client wished to avoid problems with the federal government, so she wanted to amend her federal income tax return to indicate the income. At my suggestion, she amended her return to report the $35,000 as income from "retropuntal funding." A "retropunt" is a kickback. To this date no questions have been asked by the Internal Revenue Service. The statement was an accurate report, but it profundified the facts by the use of one Borenword. The function was preserved, but its effect was a dispersality of interpretation.

Fuzzification, a management tool which is less functionally oriented than profundification, can be found in all organizations. Fuzzifying brings together both vertical and linear mumbling, but unlike profundifying, it is not used to express accuracy but to build linguistic escape from potentially embarrassing situations. For example, when you wish to establish goals or objectives to include in a report to the board of directors or the stockholders, the goals should be fuzzified. That is, you should express them in terms that seem to be clear and precise but, within their harmonic modalities, are analytical variables.

As an outstanding corporate executive or agency head, for example, you should use a few words and phrases that can be subject to multiple interpretations in the future. As a politician, the mastery of fuzzifying is absolutely essential for the maneuvering room needed during campaigns. Regardless of the meandering flow of events, the competent fuzzifier can interpret his or her performance as measured against the established goals to be whatever is best at the time the performance is under review by having had the foresight to assure the adjustivity of interpretation by the original fuzzification. Clear and precise terms leave no maneuvering room, but fuzzification assures success through the built-in adjustivity of interpretation. Professors of English may lash out against fuzzification, but they really don't influence corporate policies or political processes anyway. They rarely own much stock in corporations, and few vote.

The language of lawyers is noted for verbal stretch and profound floatational bloatum as they seek the fuzzifications of concurring precedents. Television moneyvangelists fuzzify in heavenly-oriented words, and they shift into whinal tones as they reach with outstretched arms to seek love offerings from the people. Doctors are masters in fuzzifying diagnostic projections, and their prescriptions are enscribbled for partial comprehension by pharmacists. Politicians embellish their speeches with rhetorical snortations and roundness of vowels, but their fuzzification skills often remain at a lower level of excellence. In whatever arena you may find yourself, you should project the image of being a knowledgeable leader by fuzzifying with words and terms which denote a pragmatic approach to issues. Prudent reasoning; realistic decision-making; effective institution building; profitable portfolio management; viable constructs; feasible qualitative-quantitative interfaces; sensible proposals; practical parameters; bottom line efficacy; sound inputs; and credible strategies. By fuzzifying ideas or proposals in down-to-earth terms, you will establish yourself as a no-nonsense leader. It is important that subordinates as well as superiors think you "have your feet on the ground." If you have your feet on the ground, you won't have far to fall.

Not all fuzzifications are aimed at image enhancement; many are used simply for survival in an organization. Through my many years of research in the language of bureaucracy, one of the most abstructional fuzzifications came from the director of a Reorganizational Task Force for the U. S. Social Security Administration. He wrote about the new organizational goals. "This delineation and separation of the systems and procedures functions in the transferred components and their proper relocation in the OOPP require further detailed analysis. Also the appropriate locations of certain other specific functions which are currently located in the systems and methods area require further evaluation. These remaining subsidiary issues are under active consideration by the Reorganization Task Force and further decisions in these areas will be announced with the issuance of subsequent reorganization memoranda."*

I have never been able to determine the final fallout of the task force, but results are rarely a measurement of success. Whatever the task force may have concluded, I am relatively confident that the status of the nation's social security system would be safer in the hands of the task force than in the hands of today's members of Congress.

The Pentagon is renowned for its fuzzifications. A member of Congress accidentally read a line in an appropriation bill providing funds for an "enhanced radiation device." It was a fuzzification for the neutron bomb that would kill people while preserving buildings and equipment. In one of

---

*Reorganization Memorandum No. 3, from Milton R. Johnson, Director, Reorganization Task Force, U. S. Social Security Administration, date 1/20/79.

the Pentagon documents, bullets were listed as "kinetic energy penetrators;" war was "violence processing;" and peace
was "permanent pre-hostility." Bombing was called "target
servicing;" and dropping paratroopers into Grenada was a
"predawn vertical insertion." Politicians, Pentagon officials
and pontificating pundits accepted "ethnic cleansing" as a
term for genocide. They called civilian casualties "collateral
damage" and the destruction of military targets "degrading
capabilities." No one suggested a need for linguistic cleansing. If you have access to Pentagon reports, study them for
emulation. If you do not have access, write to the General
Accounting Office in Washington, and ask to be put on their
mailing list to receive reports of studies in progress. The
reports will include examples from the Pentagon and other
executive agencies.

Remember that the theme of communication is less
important than the artistry with which the words are used.
Rhetorical artistry reigns supreme in the aesthetics of the
bureaucratic art, and both profundifying and fuzzifying
can bring you success as well as a great sense of satisfaction at having said little or nothing . . . but having said it
with style!

Trashifying, Bloatating, and Globating

An effective politician or bureaucrat can develop a
position paper in any professional jargon on any subject
with any bias in a very short time. Position papers should
be fuzzified, but some minor information may be presented as long as it includes interpretive adjustivity that can
favor the old, the current, or a possible new position of the
originator. Properly written, position papers can serve as a
yawl in institutional life. Politicians and bureaucrats need

to be sensitive to the changing winds that can help carry them toward their goals.

Where are some of the sensitivities and skills that writers of position papers or campaign documents must have if they are to be successful?

Trashifying is a simple but often overlooked technique of orbital enrichment. It is based on the use of irrelevant data, maps, charts, graphs, and other material to lengthen a report. Executives in most bureaucracies are more impressed by the weight of the report than by the weight of the logic it contains. Successful politicians know that the first page of a position paper should express what he or she wants to say. The typical recipient of such a paper usually assumes that the balance is supportive material, while it is primarily a series of impressive trashifications.

While many political trashifiers begin to believe their own trashifications, bloatators rarely do. Bloatating a position paper involves puffery similar to trashifications but it is oriented toward stroking the prejudices and political biases of those to whom the paper is directed. Bloatating is puffery by inflatuation whereas trashifying is a more straightforward use of irrelevant materials. Seasoned bloatum, the puffery and strokalities of the puff piece, may produce harrrmphal gases that can disturb the political arena. Politicians should open the presentation of a position paper or any other marginal pronouncement with one or more "harrrumphs" to clear any effervescent impediments.

The value of globating is recognized by even the most inexperienced politician, but it is a skill that needs professional honing. Globation, the presentation of the biggest of the big pictures, permits speakers to go beyond speaking in circles. Circles are flat, unattractive, 360-degree planes, whereas globations are global in nature... fulsome, volumetric, multipositional instruments of communications. Changing one's position by 180 degrees is often effective, but it is still planal, not global. When a skilled globator globates, there are no corners into which the globator can be backed.

When one masters the art of globating, the need to know the nitty-gritty of issues is no longer necessary. In the Congress, for example, the politician testifying before a committee is usually an accomplished globator who is flanked by one or more nittigrittifiers who can feed useful details when they may be needed. The members of the committees, being globators themselves, rarely press a political colleague for a clear answer or a firm position until the nittigrittifiers can perform their quiet shufflistic responsibilities. That is, until they can slide a memorandum across the table to the boss who is testifying. In fact, the committee members are usually fed their questions-to-ask by their own sets of nittigrittifiers.

LANGUAGE

The Language of Power

Words can be used as the toga of power . . . the rhetorical robe of authority . . . the majestic and unassailable garment of flowing power that brooks no challenge, and tolerates no confrontation. Genuine possessors of power can throw words with random and arrogant forcefulness, or they can quietly and confidently select the words of soft but precise direction. Insecure possessors of positions of power, however, may have a weak grasp of the power that they should command but do not. Such marginal holders of power must master the special language of power in order to protect their position, and inspire some element of subservience from subordinates.

A marginal leader must reject the soft syllables that may convey an easy and benevolent approach to subordinates. A kindly attitude projects the image of weakness. A weak leader who wishes to appear to wield power must use forceful language, not the soothing and beautiful language of the poet or the philosopher. Hard syllables must dominate the selection of words, and authoritative pronouncements must tumble with p-popping consonants and trumpeting phonics.

Most successful politicians know that words of Anglo-Saxon descent are more powerful carriers of power-oriented messages than are those of Latin descent. They are the harsher words such as *hang, forbid, bloody, foe, angry, and drunkard. Hang* sounds heavier than *suspend, forbid* more commanding than *prohibit, bloody* more gory than *sanguinary, foe* more antagonistic than *adversary, angry* more furious than *irate*, and *drunkard* more sloshed than *inebriated.*

Whereas Anglo-Saxon words have not grown beyond the simple terms of a mundane and combative world, Latin derivatives have flowered and prospered. They are easily fuzzified, and they are soothing, poetic, and peaceful in impact. They trip easily from the tongue and permit a mind to function with minimal stress. There are times when competent leaders may wish to use soothing language that can tranquilize their listeners rather than stir them with such emotions as anger or fear. Politicians of marginal power use the *words* of power to project an *image* of power. They should know how to project a take-charge profile as they prod for purposeful pursuits.

A meek and mousy person can learn to control a meeting and thrash it into shape by using thundering con-

---

ROSTRATE

To thunderate from a rostrum in a manner that optimizes flourishes and tonal patterns while minimizing transfer of information. Extended rostration often leaves listeners in a state of mental prostration. The prostration does not result from attentively listening to a flow of thoughts but from the search for a thought that may be hidden in the rostration.

---

sonants, hardened syllables, and directive gestures. Such a weak leader should take advantage of the natural withdrawal tendencies of subordinates who may be present in the meeting. For example, a question will rarely be asked when the leader furrows his or her brow, juts the jaw forward, and poses the crisp query, "Any questions before we adjourn?" Participants in meetings are always eager to escape, and a poser of a question who postpones adjournment runs a high risk of engendering the wrath of the leader as well as the disdain of colleagues who are already crouched for the escape.

Politicians and bureaucrats use control-oriented questions or concluding comments to strengthen their respective positions of authority. "I assume we are all in agreement . . ." Subordinates know that superiors, no matter how basically mousy they may be, do not like having their assumptions questioned. Subordinates also know that mousy superiors may occasionally blunder into making a decision that can be dangerous, and they therefore accept the wordalities and posturings of the superiors.

"If there's no disagreement, ..." People who disagree are troublemakers, and troublemakers are rarely promoted. "Now, I know there are some who will say ..." "Some" indicates <u>outsiders</u>. Only <u>insiders</u> who are team players will prosper in any organization. "There are a few inexperienced people who . . ." In such a framework, inexperience may be equated with stupidity, but most stupid people are not stupid enough to want to be a part of such an equation. "Until our next session," A welcome prelude to physical and mental (sic) release!

Napoleon Bonaparte observed, "The great difficulty with politics is that there are no established principles." He was wrong. The fact there are no established principles is the established principle. "In politics," he said, "an absurdity is not an impediment." Aha! In this he was correct. Absurdity, stupidity, and ignorance are not impediments to leadership as long as the language of power roars from the executive throne. The image of possessed power can be strengthened through a forceful flow of consonants that crash through a conversation or harangue with the clear and crafty clattering of thunderous roars. 'Tis known by all wise and successful weak-kneed leaders that language and image are the reality of corporate as well as political life.

At the turn-of-the-millennium, the so-called postmodern language of academe has emerged as a special style of protection . . . protection provided by abstruction. That is, the language is so abstract that listeners or readers cannot be certain of the subject of a presentation. For example, quotidian projections of abstructional constructs can be appositional in nature while simultaneously being deliquescent in its impactual heteroretrogressivity. Various styles of presentation can be effective: professorial pronouncements, bureaucratic fuzzifications, clergical theotonalities, judicial bidirectives, and political heteropreclusionaries. Pomoabstructions, which are simply standard abstructional approaches, are protective, not communicative.

Postmodern mumbling is so abstructional in nature it will not be accepted in legislative halls for any extended period of time. On the other hand, saying nothing but saying it with style will be acceptable in the political market place as long as a few meaningful words are used as commonplace linkages. Whatever you so, do not try to sell ineffable ideas . . . ideas that Plato would describe as being above the descriptive level or within easy comprehension. Plato's ineffability will not sell in the political arena. Therefore, you should drivelate your fuzzifications with creative mumbles that cause people to think they might understand you. Mumblesce and prosper.

The Language of Subservience

Some people ooze to the upper echelons of organizations by guile and sly maneuvering, while others make it in a single political leap. Some rise by the power of marginal wisdom. Some may even learn of their responsibilities, perform their duties and provide the effective leadership that surviving organizations must include somewhere in their senior executive structure. There are many ladders to the top --- some with well-worn rungs, others with rungs still shining with varnish that defies the step of timid souls, and there are a few ladders that lean with the curious tilt of a taunting challenge.

People at the top of all organizations want to stay at the top. They want to enjoy the comfort of their contoured executive chairs. For the vast number of life's strugglers, however, the upper levels of organizations are less to be sought than to be understood, accepted and patronized. Understanding the ways of those on top is basic to knowing when to assume a normal profile and when to residuate into a low profile with professional skill. This is essential to being satisfied with one's less exalted but more secure status. Patronizing the holders of power is a key to job security, improved benefits, and amusement in watching the passing parade above.

It is by patronizing those on top that the use of adjustively subservient language comes into its own. Subservient language is a symphony of melodious sounds and gestures that educe the comforting of music without purpose, tonal eloquence without message and a sense of well-being without basis.

Subservient language assures superiors that nothing disruptive is taking place among subordinates. It is the cat-like purring of "mmmms" and "ah's" that indicates concurrence in whatever direction a staff meeting may be drifting. It is also the linguistic tail-flipping as subordinates fingertappingly announce their presence but do not require either response or recognition. It includes the careful selection of words and phrases that are requisitioned from the inventory of soothing syllables, tranquil tones, and melodious mumbles. The wordational strings of subservient expressions may be punctuated with some technical terms, but the key lies in the acquiescent tone.

EGOFLECT

To genuflect and make other physical gestures and tonal expressions of subservience that stroke, massage, and otherwise inflate the ego of the person to whom the egoflection is being directed. Egoflection blends well with toadalities (expressions of one person's toadiness to another). Egoflection is found everywhere, but it is particularly evident in the executive suites of large corporations, in legislative offices, and in all environs of the performing arts.

Body language adds emphasis to the tonalities that are projected toward the executive throne. Simple physical expressions should be practiced before a mirror: Facial posture of neutral stupidity. A forward tilt of the head with the eyes wide open and peering upward. One lip over the other, perhaps a mix of upper and lower dominance. Hands clasped at mid-rotundity. Creative techniques can be developed to suit the individual subservient.

Some subordinates who use meetings to indicate their toadiness are the acquiescing posicators. Posicators are those who wish to make long and marginally relevant comments in the form of a question. It is a simple way of signaling subservience while surfacing to the attention of the audience. Though found in corporate and governmental organizations, posicators most often perform in professional conferences, PTA meetings, and meetings of learned societies.

More common in annual conferences of senior executives, annual sales meetings, and faculty sessions are mid-level drivelators. In the language of subservience, nothing is as satisfying as the droning articulation of a skilled drivelator who produces drivel with eloquence. It is not disruptive; it fills holes in the agenda; and it gives the presiding officials an opportunity to shuffle their notes while determining what to do next. There is no sound worse, however, than the grating and irritating tones of an unskilled drivelator. Beginners in drivelation should practice in private before going public. Otherwise bright careers can be zilchified into a retrofittal clunkation through premature drivelation.

Politicians who survive and thrive never appear to the public to be subserviating to another politician or anyone else. Subservience, for a politician, is to be expressed quietly. In the Congress, Speakers, President Pro Tems, party Majority Leaders, and others who are the keys to the passage of legislation or appointments to committees are accustomed to the quiet but dependable subservience of politicians. Lobbyists and bureaucrats also know how to play the game.

The bottom line of the subservient practitioner is to

express readiness and eagerness to be a wallowing toady.
A bag carrier, yes; a whistle blower, no. This is the basis
of the tote-'nt-toot rule of survival. Toadies tote, but don't
toot. Politicians may blather, but not lather.

TOADALITY

A word, action, or other expression by which a toady expresses his or her
toadiness. Toadality involves the expression of extreme subservience, and it
is normally directed to persons in positions of great power or wealth, real or
imagined. A toadality may be a nod-and-smile genuflection combined
with a slight secondary hand salute. It may be a quick rush to
step aside or to scramblingly rush to pick up a dropped
item. It may be an echoing grunt that
punctuates agreement to some
marginal thought. The range
and style of toadalities
are limited only by
the creativity of
the toady.

CRISIS MANAGEMENT

Intervoidance, Committees, and Bladderations

Whether it be the national Ship of State foundering
in stormy seas or a local enterprise in a mud puddle of
threatening ripples, many people live in fear of impending
problems. This may be true of corporate, academic or governmental leaders, but it also applies to people in all walks
of life. The problems may be real, or they may be merely
image-oriented hints of disaster. Whichever it may be, it is
not wise to permit a panic attack to mar your image as a
true professional in your field. Peace of mind and organizi-
ational tranquility can be achieved by mastering the con-

cept of interface avoidance   . . . dodging confrontation.

What should you do when you sense a problem coming your way? Immediately residuate! That is, quickly assume a very low profile. Residuation is related to residuum, the last remaining particle, and the position is the lowest of low profiles. By residuating, you may be below the level of free-flying problems in search of a landing place. Residuation, a first cousin of dynamic inaction, may be enough to avoid career-endangering confrontation.

If you think simple residuation is not enough, however, you can also hunkerfy. Hunkerfication, discussed earlier, is a higher extension of an enhanced, high-tech residuation. As a psychological crouch, it can help you shift from mental neutrality as you make an effective career leap. Flexible forward leaps or side-jumps should not be made prematurely. Be patient. Remember, while patience may be a value to a philosopher, it is a process to a corporate, academic or governmental practitioner of the survival arts. Hunkerfying in an untimely manner may cause you to glide to safety with the squattistic profile of a chicken. Implemented at the appropriate time, a successful hunkerification should give you a sense of joyous relief and a confident eagerness to soar to new heights of satisfaction with eagle-like grace.

If your psychological make-up is such that your spine still tingles with fear as you execute a hunkerfication, it may not be the only way of achieving security.

Provided residuating and hunkerfying still leave you with a sense of impending danger, look for other available ways to postpone problem confrontation. Delay can be a great friend. Should you need a relatively short delay, ask your lawyer or your organization's Office of General Counsel for an opinion on some minor question. If you need more time, follow up by asking a "What if . . . " question with several variables added to the original question. All lawyers enjoy the game of delay. Extended delay is an easy and acceptable means of strengthening their positions in organizations or adding to their billable hours.

If you need even more time to get your house in order or to disperse the possible impact of a crisis, appoint two or three study committees to analyze a problem. By appointing study committees, you can give some dissident or subordinate groups within the organization the feeling they are involved in the decision-making process. Thus, the image of team work can provide a warm glow of satisfaction among the participants, without disrupting your own plans. Should your position not be high enough to directly appoint committees, simply suggest the idea to your superior, and usually it will be accepted without question.

If possible, appoint Co-Chairs. Encourage the Co-Chairs of the committees to establish several subcommittees, a number of review committees and two or more survey committees. In this manner the review committees can review the reports of the original committees, and the survey committees can make surveys of the reports of the review committees which have reviewed the studies of the original committees. The committee process can delay a decision or action for at least ten years. By that time, no one can remember the original question, and the passage of time would make it moot anyway because of the changes in circumstances that ten years would bring.

The general public thinks of committees as problem-solving entities, but they are really problem-avoidance mechanisms. If you study a problem long enough, it may go away. The problem may have passed its prime and quietly drifted into oblivion. Committees are not established to develop alternative courses of action or to seek solutions. Committees are growth hormones which fatten the body politic. Carelessly appointed and haphazardly placed committees can sloppiate the structure. Just as an overweight man can pull in his paunch as he approaches a crowded swimming pool, so also can the image of an organization be enhanced by an occasional tummy- or cranial-tuck of organizational fat.

Should your organization be threatened by a significant problem or controversial issue, arrange for a professional conference to be held at some distant resort. Provide for the mornings to be free for golf, tennis, horseback riding, swimming, shopping, or relaxing massages. Keep the first two afternoon "work sessions" fairly brief, but develop a long and heavy schedule for the last day. Arrange for the controversial issue to be last on the agenda . . . shortly before concluding for a live-band dance. Provide for a leisurely coffee break prior to considering the issue. Encourage the arrangements committee to hold the coffee session in another room. . . perhaps on another floor. . . or in another building. This will maximize drop-out. Serve a great deal of very strong coffee and a few little cookies. When the participants return to the meeting, dim the lights; turn off the air conditioning; call for a treasurer's report or an economic forecast. Copies of the report or forecast with important small-print statistics should be distributed to those who returned from the coffee break. By the time the controversial issue is reached, the participants in the meeting will agree to anything you wish them to accept simply to get out of the room. In the International Association of Professional Bureaucrats, this technique is known as bladderating a meeting.

Finally, if you want to control the outcome of the meeting, don't preside. Write the minutes.

BLADDERATE

v.-To drag out or prolong a meeting until it must be adjourned to accommodate the physical needs of the participants. Bladderation is often used by those in charge of meetings . . . who withhold a vote or decision until everyone will agree to anything merely to get out of the room. Most successful practitioners arrange for a coffee break to be held prior to bladderating a meeting, and some open the meeting by a detailed treasurer's report.

LOYALTY

When hiring a staff, all politicians and bureaucrats should select the best professional men and women possible. Knowledge of job requirements, communication skills, and other general performance factors should be considered. Competency is extremely important, of course, but the most vital qualification is unswerving loyalty. To paraphrase my friend and masterful satirist, the late Laurence J. Peter, "An ounce of loyalty is worth a ton of competence."

There are many ways of evaluating potential staff members, but the most reliable in political or bureaucratic

offices is the BOPER, the Boren Personnel Evaluation
Report. From my many years of experience, I have developed the most pragmatic evaluation guide which can be
used today. My own devotion to the things of the past
inspires me to continue the use of the term *personnel*
which rings the tonal patterns of a joyous tradition.
Though I still treasure the old terms of yesteryears, the
practicality of my evaluation report is one which tran-
scends all timality barriers.

In the Old West, the man with a fast draw was
deemed the man who would best survive, but a careful
study of boot hill cemeteries and the records of main street
shootouts reveal that the most accurate shot was the real
survivor. Therefore, a man who could shoot with a modicum of accuracy and speed would be a better bodyguard
than one who could shoot with great speed and marginal
accuracy. There are always trade-outs in the shooting
business.

Similarly, the staff member who is quick-with-a-
quip may be valuable in some circumstances, but a fast lip
of a staffer often leads to problems. A staffer who is slower with a quip but more prudent in its application may
actually be the winner. This is reflected in the 1968 Boren
Advisory: *A cautious mouth gathers no foot.* If the politician is to have a foot in his mouth, it is best that it be his
own. . . placed there by his own words. Foot-in-mouth
disease should not be tolerated among staff members. It
should be avoided, but if it is to occur in a politician's
office, it should be a self-inflicted wound. This brings us
to the crux of the loyalty question. The staff member who
will take the blame for the slip-of-the-lip of the boss is the
epitome of loyalty. He should be sought, and when found,
cherished!

The Chief of Staff. Selecting the person who is to head his or her operations is the most challenging and important task of a politician or a senior bureaucrat. The loyalty issue has been discussed, but success in an office requires a competency which is the shadow of the Boss. That is, the Administrative Assistant or Chief of Staff must be able to think as the Boss thinks both in ideas and words. Such a closeness requires a personal as well as a professional relationship that is rarely achieved, but it is found where there is powerful status in position, major influence in the area represented, and longevity in office.

The chief of staff is the alter ego of the politician or the senior bureaucrat. It is the task of the Chief of Staff to be the best representative possible, but it must be shown to constituents and others in a manner which recognizes the superiority of the Boss. When needed, the COS represents the Boss before legislative committees, in political meetings, in meetings with governmental agencies and among other members of the staff. When the Chief of Staff speaks, it is the Boss also speaking. The office that is of one voice provides the strength and recognition that elevates it in the eyes of colleagues. And it quickly resounds in the views of constituents. This is good for everyone. It is important that the closeness of the Chief of Staff and the Boss remain extremely close, and for that reason the unquestioned mutual loyalty of the two is vital. Loyalty is not given; it is earned. But loyalty, loyalty, loyalty are the three most important factors in the political relationship between the office holder and the right hand person.

Boren Personnel Evaluation Report (BOPER)

As an aid to managers, BOPER is the most pragmatic evaluation guide now available for personnel evaluation. While most personnel evaluation reports are pedantic, esoteric, and based on such impractical considerations as performance or measured productivity, BOPER focuses on the factors by which the real evaluations are made. The most important of these factors is loyalty. As an aid to working-level (sic) employees, BOPER stresses the real factors by which employees are judged, and thus serves as a practical tool which may help them bubble to the upper crust of the institutional cesspool.

I. TEAM PLAY: Rate the employee on a 1-20 being the highest score.

___1. Never asks why, only how high.
___2. Accepts stupidity without question.
___3. Views all policies as guides by which to prove loyalty.
___4. Covers for the Boss during long and frequent absences.
___5. Accepts all management decisions until the Boss is about to be replaced.
___6. Effective in factalytical determinations.

II. COMMUNICATIONS SKILLS: Rate employees on a 1-10 scale, 10 is the highest.

___1. Fuzzifies objectives and interpretive reports at the drop of a memo.
___2. Profundifies simplicity with enriched wordalities. Occasionally abstructs concepts.
___3. Expands short reports by trashifying with irrelevant data, footnotes, charts, and compuslush.
___4. Projects sincerity (furrowed brow, pupillary contact, intermittant head-nods and chin-strokes).
___5. Projects an image of concern and sincerity without laughing.
___6. Appears thoughtful (with eyes open or closed). Lip-pursing, eye squintations.
___7. Avoids issues through professional drivelations and orbital dialogues.
___8. Judicially thunderates in resonant tones while maximizing pupillary contact.
___9. Articulates marginal thoughts while interdigitating simultaneously or sequentially.
___10. Mumbles without hesitation.
___11. Writes with the brevity of a clergyman and the clarity of a lawyer.

III. GENERAL PERFORMANCE FACTORS: Rate employee on a 1-10 scale.

___1. Applies the principles of dynamic inaction . . .does nothing, but does it with style.
___2. Quantifies abstract program results.
___3. Guides meetings to avoid decisions.
___4. Meets report deadlines regardless. Enriched with drivelated fuzzifications.

___5. Shuffles paper with minimal noise unless circumstances demand optimal tonal flippifications.

___6. Represents Boss or Office with harrumphal dignity.

___7. Knows where the right memos are buried; selectively surfaces those most useful at the time.

___8. Complexifies forms, charts, regulations, and other client-oriented engoosational documents.

___9. Halljogs with file folder high under one arm. Grim expression; furrowed brow.

__10. Organizes attention-diverting crises with minimal notice.

Media Specialists and Speechwriters

When a political figure hires the person who is to deal with the media, competence is a significant fact, of course. The person should be able to read, write, and know when and how to go for the jugular. He or she should be able to lurk around the watering holes of the powerful and the near-powerful in order to sop up the drippings of marginal wisdom. Watering holes bubble with political intelligence that is useful to all politicians. Many media specialists know the bartenders at the most important establishments, and they often make arrangements for a single alcoholic drink. . . with subsequent "the usual" order being understood as something non-alcoholic. Though a capacity for some alcohol may be accepted, it is preferable that the media person drink ginger ale or other non-alcoholic beverage which preserves sobriety, an inquiring mind, a good memory, and the ability to take notes with a stub of a pencil in a pocket or in the depths of a purse. Notes of key words can later be translated into a memorandum for future use.

The media person often serves as a speechwriter,

but this function is of less importance, since most politicians wander all over the semantical landscape anyway. Their speeches are noted for little organization and minimal messages. As long as the politician can skirt issues with profound profundification while interlacing the names of the key notables in the audience, the speech will be a success. An outstanding speechwriter is usually not happy when the speech is over. When the speech is delivered and the carefully written prose, the marvelous logic of concepts, and the inspirational conclusions are garbled by the inept office holder, many speechwriters head for the nearest bar. But of such is the burden of the speechwriter. Experienced speechwriters usually give up on writing memorable prose, and devote most of their time to gathering political intelligence. This the office holder can understand and appreciate, while masterful speeches are held in esteem only by political scholars and other speechwriters.

Any staff member, including an outstanding speechwriter, must avoid optimal sloshification, regardless of how understandable it may be. Sloshed staff members are known for slushmental notes and slipped lips, and they become marginally effective in an office. The politician should arrange for such a staffer to be lured away to another office. With quiet contrivance and the help of political allies, a better paying position can be found. This assures friendliness and continuing loyalty, and it opens the door for hiring a more professional and dependable person.

As a guide to evaluating an effective speechwriter, the following Rules for Speechwriters may be useful. The Rules were developed originally for my remarks to the Washington Speechwriters Roundtable.

The first rule of any speechwriter is simple: Know the audience. The chief objective of a political speech is to leave the audience with a sense of satisfaction rather than to impart information or an understanding of some elusive subject of the speech. When the speech ends, the politician should budget enough time to permit him or her to make pupillary contact and shake hands with members of the now milling-around audience.

Boren Rules for Speechwriters

1. If the speech is to be to a friendly audience, open with a few time-proven, old jokes. Friendly audiences will laugh even if they've heard them many times. Be sure they are clean jokes. Politicians should avoid smutty stories. Give the party line, and sprinkle the speech with statistics. Numbers give credibility to ignorance.

2. If the audience is an unfriendly one, use no more than one opening joke. Fill the time with boring and irrelevant statistics, perhaps unreadable slides on the national budget. Refer to favorable studies and report of echosultants who support the favorite programs of your Boss. Toward the end of the speech, add a marginal note advising your Boss to "Gather Notes." This will advise the audience the end of the speech is near. . . and it will also expedite safe departure from the platform.

3. Abstruct all controversial issues. Destroy the clarity of issues by making them so abstract they cannot be understood. (Abstraction + Destruction)

4. Globate all other issues. By globating the biggest of the big pictures, there are no corners into which the Boss can be backed.

5. Profundify or profundicate the speech. Use Roget's

Thesaurus or other language enrichment materials to make simple ideas seem very profound.

6. Fuzzify all positions, plans and objectives by using words which are subject to multiple interpretation. Fuzzification makes extensive use of multisyllabic wordations in a series. . . aka word stringing.

7. Dynamic inaction (doing nothing but doing it with style) can be applied to speaking. When your speaker has nothing to say, let him or her say it with style. Gestures, tonal patterns, and head cockeries can enrich a marginal concept.

8. If the speech is to give bad news (such as the closing of a military base), cacotonalize the speech with words that are easy for the speaker to nasalize or squeak in irritating tones, but hold fast to irrelevant words. Cacotoning causes some listeners to stop listening.

9. For powerful expressions, thunderate loudly with Anglo-Saxon words; for soothing expressions, use Latin-based words. (The Language of Power)

10. If you write marginal notes of gestures, thunderations or other instructions, make them distinct from any possible message. You don't want the Boss to read the marginal notes as part of the speech.

11. The marginal note "mumblio ad libitum" is to remind the speaker to stretch the timality by straying from the text and by "extemp" or free-style mumbling. "Mumblio sostenato" is a marginal note to remind the speaker to sustain the mumbling and then end the speech back near the subject. Mumbling can cover any ideas that may inadvertently develop.

12. Telegraph the end of the speech. Let the audience be aware of the approaching end of the speech. This

will wake them up, and it will prepare them to give the applause you desire. Remember that sleeping audiences are not disruptive but cooperative, and they deserve your consideration.

13. Conclude the speech with a series of patriotic references and a few flag-waving lines. Remember George M. Cohan's advice: "Many bad shows have been saved by the flag." Or, remember the Boren Advisory: "Stupidity wrapped in the flag will prevail over wisdom wrapped in the law."

Special attention should be given to the key role played by an effective and intelligent speechwriter. He or she may help set policy, or at least define the political position of the Boss. How? Simply by carefully writing the policy or position into the text of a speech which is to be made before microphones or cameras. Few politicians read the speeches prior to the on-the-platform presentation, and they will be committed before they realize it. Some may even read the speech prepared for them without understanding what they are reading. By that time, it is too late, and the speechwriter may have committed the Boss to a policy or a position on an issue.

Fuzzistics for a Political Speech to any Audience

If your speechwriter is ill or has quit you for better pay or a better working environment, don't panic. In an emergency, you can make an excellent non-position speech to any type of audience by using the Fuzzifier. If you need to be more specific in speaking to a particular group, merely toss in a few fuzzwords that would relate to the audience.

For practice purposes, select a phrase at random from each group. Select them in sequence from A to B to C to D. With minimal practice, you can drivelate with eloquence.

Group A

0 While we all recognize the dangers of the political developments in the Middle East,

1 In the words of the great philosopher of the 13th Century, Jeremiah Abberjabber,

2 If we are to be true to our democratic ideals, and hold our traditional values,

3 As we gather here today beneath our beloved national flag,

4 As the record has been written clearly in the footnotes of history,

5 If we are to preserve our democracy as it was conceived by our founding fathers,

6 As citizens of the most powerful nation in the world, a great freedom-loving nation,

8 Based on the most recent revelations about the United Nations,

9 Recognizing the floatational level of the current state of communications technology,

Group B

0   the spiritual subsets of the challenges facing all of us
1   the cherished cross-cultural linkages
2   the high-tech approach to philosophical motivation
3   the unifying ideals of all freedom-loving nations
4   the multiphonic tonalizers of disinformational reports
5   all our unfailing efforts in support of cognitive morality
6   the theoretical integrity of appositational factors
7   most of the priorities that fall within the parameters of a spurious foreign policy
8   we, the God-fearing people of a mighty nation
9   steadfast devotion to profitable morality

Group C

0   must expand the economic basis of job-oriented concepts for
1   should update the historical data in order to assure that renewed strategies for
2   can translateralize the idiotoxic domesticity of patriotic endeavors for
3   may result in a positive, though adjustive, modality of
4   cannot disrupt the firm morality of orbitational dynamics for
5   must reduce the multiheterocity of employment standards within
6   should retrograde the procedural abstractions of
7   should establish clearly that our flag is a symbol of
8   can transform pseudo-scientific constructs that our national security demands of
9   may bind all of our national institutions into a strong and patriotic modality for

Group D

0   the guarantee of full employment of our own people to assure security for our cities.

1   the building of more law enforcement centers, more jails, and more gas chambers.

2   the Party's mission of dauntlessly preserving the heritage of our nation.

3   the upcoming, ongoing, and, ultimately, the onstopping dynamics of peace in our time.

4   the future generations of Americans to inspire love of mother, home and heaven.

5   the honest standards of a profound image that can undergird our system of economics.

6   the academic and legal goals we seek as an adjustive view of scientific knowledge.

7   the values of our nation for which our forefathers and foremothers fought to give us.

8   the bipartisan bloatum of engoosational motivation which deliquesces from our land.

9   the adjustivity by which future historians can interpret the encoded theories of justice.

DOING BATTLE

If you are entering a campaign, discard any ideas you may have about being in an easy and polite exchange of views preliminary to decisions by the voters. It never happens. Even though you may not want to be aggressive, you should prepare yourself for a tough encounter. Be ready for personal attacks, distortions and outright lies. Determine the issues you wish to make central to your campaign, then go on the attack. Wrap the issues around the neck of your opponent, then make it into an effective

noose that you can drag to the hanging tree of your choice.
Do not be cornered into some debate or joint appearance
where he commands the physical battlements as well as
the agenda, and the audience. Control the meeting place;
if you can't control, don't go. Instead, send some junkyard
dog of a lawyer who can rip your opponent apart without
direct fallout fluttering to you.

     With control of the meeting place goes the poten-
tial of packing the front rows with your lackeys and flacks
who can make your opponent's remarks unacceptable.
Control may also include the sound system which can be
made to enrich your voice and weaken your opponent's by
frequency factoring. It may also determine the best cover-
age by both the print and the electronic media by accessi-
bility and camera angles. Take charge, and fill the meeting
place with a large and power-packed assemblage of your
supporters. It there is no such group, organize one.
Consider groups such as "The National Association for the
Defense of Homes, Churches, and Synagogues," "The
Society of Religious People for a Greater America," "The
League of Patriotic Americans" or possibly "Senior
Citizens for a Sound America." If a joint appearance is to
take place in a somewhat balanced atmosphere, be sure to
have present as many of your friends as possible. Include a
few men and women of high public visibility and wealth.
Put them up front. If their reputation is excellent, you
may help offset some of the weak spots in your own. If,
on the other hand, friends with marginal reputations insist
they want to be present, it is acceptable to include them if
you can shuffle them into a media-free corner and sur-
round them with people who are dull in demeanor as well
as attire. Whatever you do, do it with style!

     Remember that voters do not trust educated people.

They prefer the expression of "good old boy" ignorance which makes you one of them. Therefore, relax and let your natural ignorance flow with freedom and pride. If you are well educated, remember to suppress knowledge of the fact. If you are a woman running for public office, the opposite tilt is not only advised but is strongly advised. Women must be educated, but they must exercise some care in how they reveal intellectual qualities to voters. Men respect bright women, but they must not be bright and "uppity". Blustery ignorance is a man's domain, and the current predominance of men in politics reflects the national preference for flamboyant ignorance and arrogance. If there is some doubt in your mind about this, simply watch the week-end interviews and mumbles of pundits, political leaders and self-appointed arbiters of national values.

These and other sideline matters can determine the outcome of an election. Cumulatively, they could affect the winning margin of a close election.

Remember, you are not in a political battle to lose or to end in a tie. You are in it to win, so use your mastery of issues, the time and place of your thunderating oratory, and the sincerity of your commitment to carry you to victory. If your opponent tries to hit you with some no-win issue, thunder your indignation at so petty an attack. Discard his "cheap, gutter-level" attack, and throw it back in his face . . . or clearly and publicly discard to the garbage heap where it clearly belongs. Hit him with a thunderating charge of your own. "What people really want to know is. . . " From that point, you can thunderate with the language of power. Use good Anglo-Saxon words that clatter with punchy, krackling consonants. Such words go well with indignantly thundered roars of robust, vertical mumbles. Let these be the resonant fillers between your clear and precise presentation of the issues as you want them to be. Remember, vertical mumbles that embody power-packing words enable you to take charge of the battle, while you maneuver to find the final thrust that comes on the eve of the election itself. There are no plow-shares in politics.

If your opponent has an opposition research group which finds a number of skeletons in your closet, lock the door if you can do so without leaving tracks. If, on the other hand, the evidence is too overwhelming, and if too many people know about the skeletons, admit it up front. As history will reflect, it is not wise to make a clumsy attempt to settle the matter through banter, barter or retro-extortion. If it relates to a matter that could go to court, settle. Settle quickly. A costly settlement may be cheaper than the political cost of a later well-financed, expansion-ary expedition that might unveil other veils in the trevails relating to the closet(s).

If the sounds of rattling skeletons grow louder and louder, be somewhat honest about your public statements. It is not wise to raise your hand and swear to a set of minimal facts, nor is it wise to point your finger at a television cam-era, but whatever you do, do not project a pattern of disinfor-mation before a grand jury. If some legal beagle is snorting around the bushes, don't let it worry you . . . excessively.

Have your own opposition research team at work. If you find foul linen in the dirty clothes hamper of your opponent, arrange to be asked about it on some televised news show. Rise above the gutter. Don't deny the possible truth of the rumor or charge; let your opponent carry that joyous anchor. Simply proclaim that yours is a positive campaign! Of course, you should not hamper friendly rumormongers in their pursuit of equity in the political arena. While you appear to be well above the gutter level of your opponent, be as flynt-hearted as necessary.

If moneyvangelisitic harpoons come your way, throw up a barricade to your right. Rise up in thunderating indignation. Embrace all the trappings of the predominant religious pressure, but you need not go beyond the hug.

Know the issues, take charge, control the time and place of campaign battles, and roaringly thunderate your way to an inspiring victory.

THE BOREN QUESTION

Are you willing to bet your entire career on this decision?

For centuries, people been concerned with the difficulty of wringing a decision or a position out of a politician or a bureaucrat. A bad decision, once given, is even more difficult to change than to obtain. A rarity of sound, steadfast positions has caused consternation in governmental, corporate, religious, and academic institutions as well as to taxpaying citizens. The Boren Question, though not a solution, may be helpful in many circumstances. How may it apply?

Let us assume that a family, for example, moves into a new neighborhood with a freezer load of meat, and needs to have electric power immediately. It is a Thursday morning, and the applicant is told by an officious clerk that the power cannot be connected until Monday or Tuesday. How can the clerk be motivated to change his or her mind, and get the job done immediately? Try asking, "Are you willing to bet your entire career on this decision?"

A salesperson needed to make an unexpected business trip to obtain a major order from a client. He could not travel until he had the appropriate approval form cleared by underlings. The approval form for the trip was on the desk of the Deputy Associate Assistant Executive Officer who had to approve all travel, but he was away from the office on vacation. The Assistant to the Deputy Associate Assistant Executive Officer hesitated to extract the form from the basket and sign off on an approval. How could the salesman encourage the assistant to the higher assistant to approve the travel, so the matter could be placed before the big boss for final approval? He asked the Boren Question. It worked; he traveled; the order was obtained.

A visitor from another country was assaulted and badly beaten on the streets of Washington, and an officer in the protocol office of the U. S. State Department needed to advise the Ambassador representing the visitor's country of the matter. Because formal notes to foreign ambassadors normally began with the words, "I have the honor to inform Your Excellency . . .", the officer wished to change the wording. He did not feel comfortable about being "honored" to advise the ambassador that one of his countrymen had been subjected to a bad beating. How could the official in the protocol office shake loose an appropriately worded note? The person in charge of notes insisted on the standard note form. The Boren Question worked.*

The Boren Question: Are you willing to bet your entire career on this decision? Designed primarily for bureaucrat-nudging, the Boren Question is an effective weapon for many political and bureaucratic battles.

It is the Boren view that no more than once in a lifetime will a person bet his or her entire career on any single decision or position. Most often the positions will

---

*Pedro Sanjuan finally won his battle in the State Department's Office of Protocol to advise the Ambassador by writing, "I regret to inform you . . ."

be altered or qualified to avoid such a final career-betting confrontation. Those who have bet their careers in such a situation often find they no longer have a position.

What if Moses, standing on the heights of Mount Sinai, had asked God the Boren Question, would we have only nine commandments instead of ten? If Lot had been asked the question at the appropriate moment, would he have succumbed to the wiles of his daughters? "Lot, are you willing to taint your position in the Bible by what you are about to do?" Could the shock of the question have enabled him to withstand the temptation wrought by both the daughterly wiles and powerful booze?

Niccolo Machiavelli, the fifteenth century bureaucrat, was a failure. He held numerous important posts during a distinguished career in public service, but he bet his career when he put his job on the line by closely identifying himself with a political Administration. Though Machiavelli's counsel to Prince Lorenzo has survived though the ages, he clunkated when Prince Lorenzo clunkated! Though recognized by many historians and political scientists to have been a successful bureaucratic advisor, he was actually a failure. Machiavelli was exiled by the Medici. He plunged from fine wines elegantly served in crystal glasses to cheap wines inelegantly sipped directly from the bottles. He bet his career, and lost the ultimate bureaucratic test: He lost his job. Had he been asked the Boren Question at the moment of decision, he may have prodigiously pondered it long enough to have saved his job.

Consider the Trojan War. Paris, the son of the king of Troy, had carried off Helen, the wife of Menelaus of Sparta. Some 100,000 troops went to Troy where they laid siege to the city for ten years. They were not able to gain entrance to the city until Greek soldiers were hidden in the interior of a huge wooden horse. Entrance was gained, and Troy was captured, sacked, and burned. If the Boren Question had been asked by one of the gate-keeper's assistants, perhaps the gates would have remained closed, and Troy saved from conquest.

King Ferdinand V of Spain was very cool to the plea for assistance from Columbus, because his kingly efforts were directed at forming a powerful coalition in Europe. Queen Isabella gave support to Columbus. Would history have been changed if King Ferdinand had chauvinistically whirled upon the Queen and said, "Woman, are you willing to bet your entire future on the success of the Columbus scheme?" Is it not possible that Queen Isabella might have chosen a conservative response, removing the important support needed for the Columbus voyage?

When decisions were made on alternate courses to sail or different directions to take on land, would the Boren Question have altered the explorations of Vasco da Gama who found the route to India, Ferdinand Magellan whose one remaining ship completed the voyage around the world, John Cabot whose explorations established England's claim to North America, and Sir Walter Raleigh who was America's first chamber-of-commerce tourism promoter? Had the Incas in Ecuador been asked the Boren Question before filling the room with gold for ransom, would they have been conquered by the double-dealing Pizarro and his Conquistadors? Would the question possibly have prevented the Aztecs from falling to Cortes? The Mayas to the Toltecs?

Had President John F. Kennedy asked the Boren Question of Allen Dulles, then director of the Central Intelligence Agency, the decision on his first foreign policy venture might have been different. Had Dulles returned to

CIA headquarters to discuss the invasion one last time with his key advisors, would the fracasso of the Bay of Pigs invasion of Cuba, on April 27, 1961, have been avoided?

If President Lyndon B. Johnson had asked the Boren Question of his chief military advisors, "Are you willing to bet your entire future in public service on this assessment?" could the course and extent of the United States involvement in Vietnam have been changed?

If the officials of International Telephone and Telegraph had been asked the Boren Question, would the intervention in the internal affairs of Chile have taken place?

Had Jim Bakker been asked the Boren Question at the right time, would he have retained his ministry and his marriage? Had Oliver North or Elliott Abrams been asked the Boren Question in a timely manner, would each have told Congress the truth instead of lying? Had President George "No New Taxes" Bush been asked the Boren Question before agreeing to a raise in taxes, would he have been re-elected President? And think of the course of political history if President Bill Clinton had been asked the Boren Question in the heat of the moment. We may have had silence in the Oval Office instead of the Zipppp Heard Around the World!

Alas! We shall never know, but perhaps political science scholars around the world may wish to ponder these possible uses of the Boren Question. Maybe even a good topic for a PhD dissertation?

As a male politician, you may enhance the effectiveness of the Boren Question by shoving a cigar into your mouth, glowering at your target, and gutturally enunciating your words. A guttural or gruntal utterance indicates annoyance. . . and the end of patience. As a female politician, you may enhance the question's effectiveness by being studious-

ly polite. Smile with a slight trace of a grimace; open your
eyes wide and arch your brow. You may even wish to
extract your compact from your purse, check your lipstick
or hair, then, holding the compact in your hand, ask the
question. The expression of power is different between the
sexes. The male may exude the garrulousness and brawni-
ness of his dangerous ignorance, while the female may project a spidery wiliness that strikes fear into the hearts her target. Each politician should develop his or her most skillful
body language to accompany the Boren Question.

When not to ask the Boren Question

As with powerful medications, there are times and
conditions which are not appropriate for their use.
Similarly, the Boren Question has limitations.

Imagine, for example, you are driving your car
through a heavy rainstorm and, in your hurry to arrive
home, you make an illegal turn. Listening to your favorite
music on the radio, you fail to hear the wail of the policeman's siren. It is not until the flashing red lights appear
about to crash through your foggy rear window that you
are aware of being paged. You stop your car, and the tow-
ering policeman lumbers through the rain to your window.
As you hand him your driver's license, he waves off your
first words as you attempt to explain your way out of a
ticket. At that moment, you think of asking the Boren
Question. It is a very doubtful use of the question. A general rule is: Do not ask a policeman the Boren Question,
particularly if he or she is standing in the rain.

Assume you were given a ticket, and were ordered
to appear in court. In the courtroom, you find yourself one
of many people who have been waiting and listening for

hours to a long series of sad or incredulous stories being told to the judge. Your presentation to the judge should not end by asking the Boren Question.

Similarly, it would not be advisable to pose the question to a nervous robber whose gun hand appears to waver in an uncertain manner. The purpose of the Boren Question is to obtain a change in a decision or position from one that you do not want to one you do want. A waving gun in a wavering hand would symbolize sufficient behavioral authority to suggest that the gun-wielder has already made basic career decisions which would not be changed by the question being asked.

It is also inadvisable for politicians or bureaucrats to ask the magic question of voters or plain, everyday, non-voting, taxpaying citizens. Though it carries a significant force, the Boren Question also conveys an element of arrogance that may not be proper for those who ultimately foot the bills of the government. Though it may not be sincere, politicians and bureaucrats should deal with taxpayers with feigned generosity in their gentle gestures, cautious resonance in their warm tones, and apparent supplication in their disdainful demands.

Perhaps, of course, there may come a time when key decision-makers may relate the Boren Question to issues of a much broader purpose. Do we want to bet all the heritage of the past and all our hopes for the future on the course we are now pursuing? Are we, all people of the world, willing to bet our lives on the sustaining force of apathy? Are we to accept the societal drift until it is too late for the Boren Question to be of value? The roaring guns and the hissing missiles of war? The moans of pain? The silence of death?

Dominoes, anyone?

PART THREE.

Jim Boren's

BIBLE
for Politicians

"The Powers-That-Be took the mud of the gutter, the waters of the still, the gases of the air, and they formed a Politician."

Illustrated by Bill Rechin

113

The Pursuit of Political Wisdom and Inspiration

In our search for answers to profound questions, we often study the works of great poets, philosophers and religious leaders. We read the translations of works originally written in hieroglyphics, Sanskrit, Greek, Hebrew, Latin, Chinese and Legalese. We read translations of translations and we scan the collections of abridged judicial decisions. We seek peace and inspiration from great composers whose music helps us reduce discordant sounds from political life. In times of great desperation, we even study the Biblical quotes which we have learned at the knees of our speechwriters.

In my long quest for the adjustive wisdom of the ages, I prodigiously pondered the eternal vagaries of political life. I dreamed about dynamic inaction, and I meditated about the nondirectiveness of orbital dialogues. I contemplated the fuzzifications of viable options, plausible deniability and creative zilchifications. Though it was a difficult search, it was also a rewarding one, for I was inspired to enter into a realm of spiritual dispersality.

Floating through both turbulent and tranquil skies, I began to think in profound terms as I searched for wisdom which I could share with current and future politicians. Sailing both on calm and stormy seas, I rearranged the constructs of my searching soul in order to be open to all infusionable concepts that I could accept with ineffable clarity. I opened my heart, mind and soul to all the insights that I could assimilate into every part of my being . . . an osmotic translateralization for joyous sharing. And, now, as I pause in the great parking lot of life's mountain top, I turn to the language of King James to share with politicians and bureaucrats the wisdom I have trapped through my long journey.

Chapter 1:

IN THE BEGINNING . . .

In the beginning, the Powers-That-Be created government and its institutions, and the government was with minimal form and void. And the Powers-That-Be caused the foundations of the government to be half-cracked, and they called the foundations Politics.

The Powers-That-Be took the mud of the gutter, the waters of the still, and the gases of the air, and they formed a Politician. They shuffled into his heart the spirit of self-interest, and the Politician became a reigning thing.

And the Powers-That-Be said, Let there be red tape, and there was red tape; and the Powers-That-Be saw the red tape, and it was good.

And the Powers-That-Be said, Let there be words, and there were words. And they said, Let the words be formed into languages; and the Powers-That-Be heard simple words being used to communicate thoughts and exchange information.

And the Powers-That-Be said, Let there be Politicians and lawyers from whom languages canst become drivelated into profundified form and nondirective communications; And let the abstractional qualities of nondirective communications giveth expression to the marginal thoughts of slushmental thinkers; and it wast so.

And behold! The Politicians and lawyers brought

forth their own words, and they didst produce them in great abundance. And the Politicians' and lawyers' words translateralized abstructional concepts with much floatational bloatum which didst orbitate with nondirective expressions of marginal thoughts. And the words didst flow to words, wool didst cover the eyes, patriotic hype didst dull the ears, and idiotoxic concepts didst shroud the mind. And the spirit of phoniness continued to squaggle across the face of the earth.

The Powers-That-Be then planted a garden on the left bank of budgetary irresponsibility and on the right banks of fiscal idiocy; and there they put the Politician up the creek with no mental paddle of his own.

And out of the gardens, the Powers-That-Be made to grow flexible trees that wouldst bend with the winds; and they caused to flourish the entangling vines of red tape that came to bind all things into a single, pulsating mass.

And they gave the Politician many eggs; and most of the eggs were hatched into cackotonal turkeys of marginal leadership.

And the Powers-That-Be didst command the Politician, saying, of every constraining power thou mayest twiddle freely: But of the power of action, thou shalt not partake: for action breeds mistakes, and mistakes causeth careers to clunkate.

Therefore, sayeth the Powers-That-Be, thou shalt apply the Boren Principle of Dynamic Inaction: When thou doeth nothing, doeth it with style.

And the Powers-That-Be saw the Politicians doing nothing but doing it with style; and they sayeth: It is not good that the Politician is alone. We shall give him some companions. And the Powers-That-Be caused a deep but normal sleep to fall upon the Politician. And whilst he slept, they took a half neuron from the Politician's brain,

leaving half therein, and from the half neuron, they fash-
ioned bureaucrats and sheepal taxpayers.

And thereafter the Politician sought to cleave unto
the bureaucrats. But 'tis known that bureaucrats make
poor lovers, because they want to make feasibility studies
at every step. Then didst the Politician cleave unto the
taxpayer, and they were one flesh. And whilst they were
in deep sleep following the one-fleshness, the Powers-
That-Be looked upon them and said, It is good.

And it came to pass that the Powers-That-Be caused
the Politicians and the taxpayers to multiply through many
begattings. For verily, such is the nature of politics that
Politicians rarely haveth sex with one another, for when
Politicians doeth what they do, they doeth it to the taxpayers. And the politicians didst prosper throughout the land.

Wordfool Leadership

Now it is known that when the Politicians and their
handmaidens, the Bureaucrats, were children, they spake as
children; they thought as children. When they were elected
or appointed to High Office, they became Special, and
though their thoughts remaineth steadfast, they cast aside
childish words and spoke official words. Through the ages,
politicians and the bureaucrats have had a language of their
own. 'Tis a language more of sounds than of understanding.

Now all Politicians and Bureaucrats speaketh in an
unknown tongue, and they speaketh not for the understanding of the people but to wrap their concepts in robes
of wool which covereth the eyes of the people.

And it came to pass that when the Politicians and the
Bureaucrats spoketh with mighty words, they didst <u>thun-
derate</u> those words with the roaring authority of the ram's

117

horn. Yet beneath the sounds of the trumpeting horn, there
lieth only the real power of snap-crack-and-pop.

*But the image of power is often more powerful than
power itself.*

Now the Politicians shareth their trumpets with the
Bureaucrats, and they didst blow them often and mightily.
For 'tis the nature of Politicians and Bureaucrats to blow
their own horns.

The trumpeters in the diplomatic unit spake of <u>killing</u>
as "unlawful or arbitrary deprivation of life," and the trumpeters in the citadel of the military spake of <u>peace</u> as "permanent pre-hostility" and bullets as "kinetic energy penetrators."
<u>Combat</u> wast to be known as "violence processing"; <u>civilian
casualties</u> among thine enemies wast profundified as "collateral damage"; <u>being fired upon by one's own comrades</u> wast
known as "friendly fire"; and <u>those who were hit</u> by the
"friendly fire" became known as "friendly casualties." <u>Trying
to decide what to do next</u> wast announced as the development
of a "scenario dependent strategy." And the first draft of
the strategy wast written with a "portable handheld communication inscriber" that cameth from a box labeled <u>pen-
cils,</u> and <u>genocide</u> wast known as "ethnic cleansing."

Once again the Politicians blew their trumpets, and
there went out from the keeper of the budgetary semantics a
trial decree that there shouldst be a tax increase. And the people, knowing the meaning of a <u>tax increase,</u> shouted and cried,
for taxes were already round about them in much abundance.

Then didst the politicians change their notes, and
they tooted their trumpets for a <u>revenue increase.</u> A few of
the taxpaying goats of the field and the sheep of the pastures kneweth not that a revenue increase wast truly a tax
increase, so they accepteth the new wordalities with tranquil demeanor. But most kneweth that though the notes
were changed, the tune remaineth the same.

Chapter 2:

THE GAME OF POLITICS

Knoweth thou that the game of politics is not as the games of baseball, basketball, tennis, golf, and track events. For they fall somewhat within the ancient and fading code that says it matters not who wins, but how one plays the game.

But the game of politics is like the game of hockey, football, boxing or soccer where the manner of playing stirs emotions, breaks bones, sheds blood, and feeds the sanguinary lust of clashing gladiators and shrieking fans.

And, as it has been known through the ages, the game of politics has no tie. . . no relationship. . . no similiarity to the game of chess. For the game of chess requires deep thought and it requires the development and execution of primary, secondary, and tertiary strategies. For 'tis known among scholars that ignorance, stupidity and public apathy serve as the playing arena for the game of politics.

Therefore, if thou wouldst win in the game of politics, thou shouldst know the limits of the laws relating to parties, elections, and campaign extortion, for you cannot develop strategies for evasion if you don't know which limit to skirt. . . and which evasion is worth the risk. To fulfill the profitsy of a rich career, thou must develop thy team for the optimal gathering of intelligence, not only

about your enemies, but also about your friends. For verily, your friend of this day may be your enemies of the next
day, or the next week, or at any time before you can with-
draw with a wealth of happiness. If thou art to be one of
the wise and cunning old men of the political game, you
must know where the evidence and the record of shocking
sleazality are hidden. And thou shouldst be able to pull
forth from the depths of your archival vault the evidence
appropriate for the moment. Then thy evidence can be
flashed with a friendly smile. For friendly flashing of
gotchadata can be one of your most powerful plays in the
great game of politics.

But the revelation of gotchadata should only be
made when the stakes aren't worth the play. Thy protago-
nists may also know the game, and may share their own
gotchadata and their other treasures with friendly, knowledgeable, and motivational fundspersons. If the stakes are
not sufficient for the use of the gotchadata, then you
should select one of thy arms bearers to embark upon the
mission of a miniflash of minihints.

If the minihints of the miniflash prove to be insuf-
ficient and prove to be a clunkational error in strategy,
blame thy arms bearer for having made a grievious error.
For the arms bearers should know their own roles in thy
game. For this is the nature of the political game.

If you know the score, you should be a master of
the selected play, and your playcard should be filled with
many options.

Therefore, if thou wouldst win in the game of politics, know that success is built upon escalating emotions,
clashing bodies, shrieking tonalities, and greedal conquest
in the arena of public apathy. And the greatest of these is
greedal conquest.

Chapter 3:

COMMANDMENTS FOR POLITICIANS AND BABYKISSERS

Now therefore hearken unto the laws and advisories which are given ye by the Powers-That-Be that ye may survive. . . yea, even thrive . .. in the world of politics and bueaucracy.

Though they may not be written upon tablets of stone, yet shouldst they be written as fires in thy heart, as regulations in thy files, and as crib notes on thy cuffs.

Now these are the commandments, statutes, regulations, and advisories that thou shalt keep that thou may prosper mightily upon the face of the earth.

1. Thou shouldst not threaten, but honor, anyone who roosteth above thee on the organizational chart.
2. Thou shalt not have any goals before the goals of power, greed, and survival.
3. Thou shalt not covet thy neighbor's office, neither shalt thou covet thy neighbor's chair, his yes-servant, his coffee maker, his gofer, or his toady unless thou shalt have the skills and contacts to taketh them with minimal risk.

4. Thou shalt not jump until thou hath found a safe place to land.

5. Thou shalt not argue with stupid people who may knoweth more than thou knoweth, for a cautious mouth gathereth no foot.

6. Thou shalt not incite progress; yet neither shalt thou always preserve the status quo, for even the status quo may be too progressive.

7. Thou shalt not remember thy promises, nor keepeth notes of thy promises.

8. Thou shalt not implement sexual harassment, nor overly plunge thy zipper; For sexual harassment and overly plunged zippers canst be the undoing of a career.

9. Thou shalt not speak in simple language, for defuzzified clarity of communication leaveth thee no maneuvering room.

10. When in charge, ponder; when in trouble, delegate; and when in doubt, mumble.

Commandments for Babykissers

Knowest thou that the art of kissing babies is an ancient and respected form of communication that the unheralded chroniclers of political history traceth to the city of Enoch which was named after Enoch, the first son of Cain who was the first son of Adam and Eve.

Knowest thou also that in the days of Cain there came forth four flushers who wouldst flush the birds of the air rather than worketh the oxen of the fields. And 'tis known from the winds of the trees, the birds of the air, and the snakes in the grass and other well-informed sources that one of the four flushers didst seek the praise and approval of Cain and Cain's wife.

Though his name be joyously lost to history, it wast he, the first of the four flushers, who didst kiss the Baby Enoch who was the light of the eyes of Cain and Cain's wife. The first of the four flushers didst gain a favored place at the table of Cain's household. He giveth not but receiveth much; he sayeth not but speaketh much; he worketh not but appeareth to worketh much. He took unto himself the cloak of the Politician.

Therefore, if thou wouldst find a favored place at the bountiful tables of the mighty whilst thou worketh not, thou shouldst master the art of baby kissing.

Knowest thou that anyone canst kiss babies but only a Politician canst kiss babies in manifold numbers and gaineth the votes of mothers. If thou wouldst reap the fruits of baby kissing, thou shouldst abide by the wisdom of generations of political puckerers.

1. Thou shouldst not kiss a baby unless thou first asketh permission of the baby's mother. If the mother responds to your "Mayest I?" with a smile, thou shouldst firmly but gently picketh up the a baby with caution and smiling reverence. Then shouldst thou kisseth the baby gently on one cheek.

2. Whatsoever thou doest, thou shouldst not kiss a baby whose mother stands taller and broader than thee, who giveth thee only marginal permission, and who holdeth the baby in a firm clutch. For verily, thou wilt gain no vote by vigorous grapples, tugs, and pulls at a well-clutched baby.

3. Thou shouldst not kiss a baby until thou hast appraised the face of the baby. If it is clean, thou shouldst kiss the baby's cheek, gaze smilingly into its eyes, and returneth it to its mother.

4. Thou shouldst not kiss the face of a baby whose nose blubbereth or whose face beareth the dry marks of past blubbereths, for such kisses canst lead thee to post-nasal drip and blubbering speeches. Thou shouldst giveth such babies near-kisses over the tops of their heads, and smilingly declareth them to be cute.

5. Thou shouldst not kiss babies whose swaddling clothes are overly damp or otherwise fulsome inasmuch as thou mayest foul thy shaking hand or marketh thy clothing.

6. Thou shouldst not kiss groups of babies, for multiple kisses loseth their effect, and they may lead thee more rapidly along the path of measles, mumps, and other abominations.

7. Thou shouldst not drop babies thou art kissing, for surely, dropped babies will gain thee no votes.

8. Thou shouldst not approach a sleeping baby, for the mothers of sleeping babies who art awakened can become as snarling cats or hissing snakes. Sleeping babies conveyeth possible votes, but crying babies conveyeth no votes.

9. Thou shouldst not kiss babies who cometh from the camp of thine enemy, for verily, they may bite.

10. Thou shouldst not kiss babies who are near or past the age of puberty.

To succeed as a politician, thou must be able, with catlike precision, to cover thy scandals in the sands of time.

Chapter 4:

LESSONS FOR POLITICAL SALVATION

If thou wouldst thrive in the realm of free enterprise politics, thou shouldst avoid leaving fingerprints upon the levers of the graft.

If thou wouldst bubble to the upper crust of partisan cesspools, thou shouldst avoid leaving DNA prints in a random fashion.

If thou wouldst build a reputation for honesty in politics, thou shouldst hire a flack who can convincingly convert a lie into disinformation, and a kickback into retropuntal funding.

If, however, despite thy best efforts and the best efforts of thy flack, thy pursuit of dollars, sex, and other objectives mayeth embarrass thee, thou shouldst proclaim thy pursuits to be in the national interest. Wrap thyself in the flag, and thunderate a sermon from the text of national security.

Remember always! A successful politician is one who, with catlike precision, canst cover his scandals in the sands of time.

If You're Going to be a Phoney, Be Sincere About It.
(*The Boren Dictum*)

Walk with happiness in thy steps, and fear not what the unknown may bring thee. For the confidence in the future canst be sure and steadfast if thou canst hold to the spirit of the Boren Dictum: If thou art going to be a phoney, be sincere about it.

Thou knoweth there art people about thee who practice phoniness as a way of life. . . but who knoweth not their phoniness. Surely theirs shall be a life of mediocre success;

For they art obvious as they hovereth around the founts of power; they art loud as they echo the unquestioned pronouncements of their superiors; and they art known by the fauxtegrity of their works.

But look thou also at those about you who art phonies and who knoweth it. They elevate the level of their success by mastering the skills, and harvesting the resources of their sincere phoniness. These shouldst be thy counselors, thy nurturers, and thy professional snugglers as the paths to political success open to thee.

As it hath been known through the ages, routine phonies fall by the wayside, and their seeds art cast upon barren places which yieldeth not for the sower. But as it also hath been known through the ages, sincere phonies worry not about inconsistencies and cancelling truths.

Nor do they bear the burdensome mental notes of what was said to whom and on what date. Or they fuzzifiest their pronouncements with words which art subject to an adjustivity of interpretation.

Aim thy words like deadly arrows at thine enemies if crisis demandeth it, or if there be no crisis, let thy words fall as the soft snow that gives beauty, serenity and tranquility to the countryside in winter.

But remember thou well, 'tis the adjustivity of future interpretation that assures survival and success. If thou wouldst attain the whole measure of the sincere phoney, thou shouldst schedule private, but daily, practice of those skills which canst develop thy latent talent into the richness of fulfillment.

Findest thou a hidden glade or a mirrored bathroom where privacy removes all constraints from thy experiments with arm-waving, finger-thrusting, head-tilting, nose-lifting, chin-stroking, lip-pursing, mouth-twisting, brow-raising, eye-squinting, bodydipping, head cockeries, assenting moans, trombonal slurring tonalities, harrrrrumphal grunts and other additive accents of sincerity.

Thou shouldst pause before all reflecting pools or mirrors where thou canst experiment with facial expressions and wordal tonalities that wouldst enrich the image of sincerity in the times of shock, amazement, concern, compassion, pain, sadness, suffering, joy, and neutral but prodigious pondering.

When driving thy chariot, sneaketh a facial expression in the rear-view mirror. When walking before shop windows, implementeth a reflective quick-glance. Thou shouldst not miss any opportunity to hone thy skills until they shalt be as message-oriented as a sharpened filet knife in the bobbitry of political life.

Knowest thou that sincere phoniness is an art that demandeth constancy of effort and steadfastness of purpose.

After thou hast perfected these enrichments, thou art ready to master the most important skill of them all: the skill of maximizing pupillary contact. When thou hast selected the person with whom thou art going to be sincerely phoney, thou shouldst stare intently and steadily into the pupil of one eye of that person.

There art no political implications as thou chooseth between the left eye or the right eye, for verily, eyes art not as wings in political tilting. Merely selecteth the eye with which thou art most comfortable.

Never shouldst thou alternate between the two eyes, for verily, it will giveth thee the image of being shifty. As thou stareth into the pupil of the selected eye, enrich the moment with facial and tonal expressions until thou canst see that thou art in control. Then shouldst thou arch the brow, become ministerial in thy tonalities, and shaketh thy head slowly up and down. When thy target respondeth with the same shake of the head, thou knoweth success.

There hath been no communication or transfer of information between thee and thy target, yet thy target hath given thee an assenting response. Victory is then truly thine.

As soon as thou hath been given the concurring nod, thou shouldst extricate thyself from the situation. Continue to maximize the pupillary contact; project a warm smile; place one hand on the shoulder of thy target; then giveth a two-hand-on-one-hand handshake. Express thy gratitude and joy in a brief but sincere. . .yea, a <u>sincere</u> mumble. Then as thou turneth to depart, thou canst break the pupillary contact. Runneth not, but moveth out as rapidly as dignity and furniture will permit.

With these skills of the sincere phoney, thou art ready to ascend with the featherheads, circle with hawks, soar with eagles, and roost with thy collegial buzzards.

Thou Shouldst Always Tell the Truth. . .
a Half-truth at a Time

Mumble thy words and fuzzify thy prouncements, O Politician, that thou mayest thrive in the urban jungles wherein the people accepteth thy words, whatsoever thy words may be, as words of political truth.

Knowest thou that a half-truth plus a half-truth canst be a whole truth; and knowest thou also that the truth shouldst be spoken a half-truth at a time. Such half-truths shouldst be spoken in thundering tones of sincerity and with great speed, for thy listeners shouldst not be given an opportunity to wonder which halves of the half-truths thou speaketh.

If thou wouldst be assured of survival in thy political career, fuzzify thy drivelations to assure adjustivity of interpretation. For verily, thou canst then translate whatsoever thou hast said to be whatever is best for thee in thy time of need.

For 'tis known in the world of politics that if thou speaketh in clear language and in precise terms, thou leaveth thyself no maneuvering room, and surely thy rumperatory foundation canst be cornered.

When thou knoweth not that of which you speak, speak only to people who art so ignorant they will accept whatsoever thou sayeth. Or, speak only to people who are so brilliant they will interpret whatsoever thou sayeth to be something that maketh sense. For verily, adjustive mumbling and fuzzifying canst contribute to thy success in politics.

Knowest thou also that though mumbling and fuzzifying mayest strengthen thy chances for success in urban jungles, the people of rural regions rarely accepteth such forms of communication. Simpler but more inquiring minds demandeth simpler and understandable language. But 'tis also known that those people of rural regions who mayest challenge unclear language canst be deceived temporarily by thunderating resonance, vigorous gestures, and facial expressions of sincerity.

Therefore, if thou wouldst succeed in politics, tarry not in rural thickets wherein simplicity demandeth and revealeth truth in a simple form, but stay thee in urban jungles. For therein sophisticated phoniness discourageth clarifying questions, and encourageth willing but unknowledgeable acceptance.

Wherein thou canst implement interfaces of multi-syllabic and multisyllabattic wordalities with thunderational resonance, theotonal beggary, and tearful cheeks, thou shouldst do so with confidence. The abstructional qualities of thy marginal thoughts shall effervesce with the floatational bloatum that inspires accepting wonderment, slushmental acquiescence, and apathetic ignorance.

Such elusive patterns of thought shall enhance thy reputation, expand thy opportunities, and fill thy pockets. Thou shalt then be known as a political farmer who plows the field, sows the seed, and reaps the harvest of truth. . . on the halves.

Behold! Though these may be words of repetitive wisdom, they are words of great wisdom that canst help thee reap the treasures of political life and imprint thy name in the pages of history.

Be Tranquil Among Liars

Struggle not against the babble of ceremonious fanatics who moneyvangelize for the false gods of personal treasure and political power, for they may endanger thy career by the solemnity of their babble, the authority of their falseness, and the vicious use of their huckstered treasure.

The fact that thou maketh the laws shouldst not stand in the way of thy warm embrace of those who violate the laws. Hath it not been shown that those who licketh the boots of liars and saluteth the flag of felony wilt prevail over the minds of apathetic citizens?

Therefore, if thou wouldst rise in the swirl of blather, babble, and hype for the preservation of thy career, be tranquil among liars and thieves. For then shalt thy grasp of treasure and power be strengthened.

Enter Not by the Kitchen Door

The leader of the political caucus raised his voice in prayer, saying: *He that entereth not by the contribution table but who slippeth in by the kitchen door, the same is an ingrate and a scoundrel; and he loveth not the New Greedocracy.*

But he who entereth by the contribution table and who giveth mightily is the investor in friendship; he shalt be known as a Patron of the New Greedocracy.

To the investor the doors shall be opened; and the friend shall hear the Politician when quiet information shall be whispereth to investors with special interests. And it shall come to pass that the Politician shall hear also the words of friends with special interests when quiet problems or fruitful information shall be whispereth in the name of beneficial friendship.

And on one of those days as he led the people in circles, and as he spoke of mother, home and apple pie, the Politician said, *Come, let us reason together, and let us share in the public trust and the public treasure, each according to the investment made in my public position. For verily, as a public servant, I shall serve or I shall service, and the degree to which I serve or service shalt be in accordance with the size of love offerings and the devotion thou showeth to my various hipful needs.*

Thy investment in our silent partnership, sayeth the Politician, *shouldst be in cash and other forms of trackless treasure, and my investment shall be in quiet but valuable information which giveth access to public treasure. Our joint venture shall assure thee protection from the intrusion of equity.*

And the Politicians and the investors didst go unto the Hill where they didst bind together in the place where pledges are given, where promises are made, and where tables covereth the transpalmations from one hand to another.

The Highest Reality of Politics

Watcheth the movement of the people; harken unto their words, their gruntifications; their songs.

Learneth the prejudices of the bigots, and fuzzify thy spoken messages to them in wordalities that hinteth thou art in agreement with them though thou are not.

For 'tis known to all political prophets that voters whose lives are ruled by prejudices art also attracted to politicians whom they *thinketh* shareth their prejudices. In the land of the bigots art the fleet of lip, the fluff of mind, and the flint of heart, but they art all to be found mightily at work fossilizing the souls of the people.

But they doeth it not in the name of bigotry, but in the name of patriotic religion or religious patriotism. For

is it not known that people heareth better than they thinketh? And if prejudices roll trippingly from the tongues of
the haters, or if they thunder from cavernous mouths
housed below the smallest minds, the timid of the land
wilt turn away, and the brazen of the bigots will deign to
reign.

For the Politicans who seeketh the votes of the bigots, searcheth for the land of the bigots. Where canst one
find the land of bigots? Canst it be found in the hinter-
lands or in the urban centers?

Knowest thou that the snobs of urban centers thinketh the biggest bigots resideth where the necks art red and
the bellies art beerable. But verily, the land of the bigots
includeth the urban centers where the martini reigneth
supreme over the daily flow of suds, and where the pan-
eled boardrooms echo the racist and sexist slurs which art
the botched elements of prejudice.

Therefore, if thou wouldst seek the votes of the
bigots, for they art many, goeth thou into all corners of the
land. For verily, there are no boundaries to the land of the
bigots, or canst they be measured by the age of the bigots.

Learneth the prejudices cautiously, and then dripple
them from thine own dry lips. . . lips parched by the vacu-
ous vacuuming search for the mental debris of the floor
and the gutter. As thou drippleth for the for-the-locality
prejudices of thy listeners, thou mayest capture their votes.

Therefore, when thou faceth a formidable opponent
in the political arena, seeketh not to surpass his knowledge
and articulation of issues, but appeal to the greater sensi-
bilities of the people. Seeketh thou the soft underbelly of
the public's fears and prejudices. Wrappeth thy combative
wrath in the armor of a patriotic defense of their prejudices while entangling thy opponent in the snares of

shared fear and nurtured hate.

With the jawbone of an ass, attack the character of thy opponent, and fear not the boundaries of truth. If thy opponent be a thoughtful person, attack him as a slothful scholar who wouldst prefer the repose and safety of a cloistered retreat to the toils and dangers of combat. If thy opponent be unsoiled and untainted with scandal, assault his innocence. Place him imcomprehensively above and beyond the trevails and hardships of the bigotted people in thy audience.

If thy opponent speaketh in positive terms, recast his words in terms which canst evoke the fears of the people. For verily, even if he sayeth not what thou sayeth he sayeth, thy wrathful thunderations wilt prevail in the minds of the miniminded voters.

Even as Lucius Paulus before thee, challenge thy opponent to leave the lofty plane of meaningful issues to descend into the gutter world of political battles. If he shouldst join thee in the gutter where thou art the master, thou canst begin to count the spoils of victory.

Survival is Essential for Happiness

Happy are the learned in law: for theirs is the language of opportunity.

Happy art they who ponder: for they shalt make no mistakes.

Happy art they who mumble their messages and delegate their problems: for they shall be managers.

Happy art the wealthy: for they shall control the earth.

Happy are the accountants: for they shalt know the score.

Happy are the warriors: for they shall serve the wealthy and their toadies, the Politicians.

Happy are the Politicians: for they shalt sup at the bounteous public breast; haveth the temporary loyalty of those for whom they canst do something; and merrily, they shalt be powerful while in office.

Happy are they who lobby for clients' sake: for theirs is protection of legal tender.

Protected are thee when taxpayers shall revile thee, and persecute thee, and shalt say all manner of evil things against thee for sanity's sake.

Rejoice, and be exeedingly glad: for great is thy power in reserve.

Ye art the law-makers of the earth: but if the law hath lost its profundification, wherewith shalt it be law? It is thenceforth good for lawyers to serve thee but to service the taxpayers. And they shouldst nourish thee, thy investors and thy friends-in-law.

And laws that art nestled in regulations and abstructed procedures canst be understood by lawyers, cryptimature bureaucrats, and Politicians. Of this is thy protection.

And the laws shalt be as beacons to all who rejoiceth whilst remaining in confusion. For though thou art not truly the light of the world, nor the beacons of hope, such must be the image thou shouldst nourish with all thy mind and thy heart.

The Dance is the Sway of the Day

Thou shouldst improve thy stamina, develop thy cultural skills, and enhance thy career if thou wouldst perfect the art of the political dance.

Knowest thou that the simple sidestep may be

effective, but its style is too simplistic to be used by the truly skilled politician.

Therefore, thou shouldst practice thy mini-leaps and thy evasive lunges; thou shouldst strengthen thy skills in pompistrutting thy way across the broad stages of narrow issues; and thou shouldst keep thine eyes in a roving mode to findeth the loopholes through which thou canst move with thundering conviction and soothing certainty. Through the tango, the twist and break-dancing, thou canst show thy flexibility in a changing world, whilst avoiding being pinned down to a fixed position.

Through the jitterbug, the bird, and the shakey-achy-breaky, thou canst demonstrate thy youth-like energy and with-it spirit, whilst avoiding inescapable corners.

Through the many moves of the waltz and the ballet, thou canst move gracefully from one non-answer to another, whilst remaining constantly on thy toes for a secure, hunkerfying profile.

But thou shouldst not dance the obvious hustle of the ancient, generation-revealing hokey pokey.

And thou shouldst avoid the bumpy humpty, and the rumperatory rhumba, the crotchifying grapple, and the undulating lambada, for they projecteth the career-wrecking image of lusty nocturnal hankipankification or nooner interlude.

Verily, Politics may be the name of the game, but the dance is the sway of the day.

Crisis Control
If your position on an issue proves to be wrong, don't change your position; redefine the issue.

When thou faceth an impending crisis, runneth not, but residuate into a low profile. Hunkerfy into a mental crouch, and prepareth to spring into whichever direction may be best for thy immediate political health.

If thy position proveth to be wrong, changeth not thy position; redefineth the issue.

When thou art confronted with the possibility of making an embarrassing mistake, knoweth there art two pathways to the implementation of an error:

(1) Dynamic action. . . actually doing something immediately. This pathway canst bring thee to such a sudden impact of error implementation that it may disturb the tranquility of the organizational entity or the body politic.

(2) Dynamic inaction, on the other hand, canst provide a safer pathway to error inplementation. Dynamic inaction is doing nothing, but doing it with style! When thou followeth this pathway, the graduality of the implementation expresseth the error through such a timality stretch that people cannot recognize the error. The mush factor canst muffle the conclusory burp of the error! Therefore, let thy political wisdom take thee along the path of dynamic inaction, for it shall lead thee safely through the land of the apathetics.

It's Hard to Look up to a Leader who Keeps his Ear to the Ground

If thou wouldst prevail as a political leader in the world of turmoil, thou shouldst think in the globalities of great events. And thou shouldst be prepared to reason through the power of weapons, for verily, men are persuaded more by the power and logistics of arms than they

are persuaded by the power and logic of reason.

Surely, idiotoxic policies shall be the last full measure of devotion. But let thy measure of devotion be wrapped in the flag of patriotism, and intoned in thy prayer. For have not all politicians, publicly and on bended knee, prayed for divine help in clobbering the Hades out of their enemies? And have not thine enemies prayed the same prayer at the same time? Dost this mean that political wars art wars between the prayers of powerful prayers? Are all wars Holy Wars?

Ponder these matters, for prodigious pondering and creative logic canst be thy mark as thou goeth forth as a leader.

And it shall come to pass that the second coming of the Big Bang shalt come from the alchemy wherein the maxipoisons of the weapons shalt prevail over the minipops of cranial power.

Therefore, thou shouldst keep thine eyes upon the horizon, where thou shalt see the stars by which thou canst guide thy footsteps along the paths on which we all must sail, as we seek the safe harbor where we canst hitch our horses, and fly on gossamer wings into the western sunset. For of such vision, such pondering of imponderables, and such intellectual drive cometh the leadership that canst build our defenses, and save our land from the evil forces of unknown enemies or yet-to-be-nourished images of enemies.

Now, go forth, win the election, prodigiously ponder, and lead us somewhere.

A DRINK, LIKE A POLITICIAN, CANST NOT BE BOUGHT, ONLY RENTED.

As it hath been known through the Golden Age, the bottom line holds that drinks are internal rentals which, in their season, must be cast from thee! Lobbyists, therefore, cannot buy drinks for thee, the Politicians, for drinks belongeth to the drinkers but for a short time. Verily, of such is the reality of drinks and the pursuit of political ownership.

And as manifold alchemists have searched mightily for the fast-buckery formula for the conversion of base metals into gold, so also have the medical bladderists searched for the secrets of the full bladder, the expanded capacity, the exit control, and the myriad intriguing mysteries of human hydraulics.

And even as the alchemists and the bladderists have searched for the unrevealed secrets of fast-buckery and human hydraulics, so have the lobbyists searched for the keys to the permanent purchase of politicians.

For is it not known that you, the Politicians, oft bear the label of your special interest? "In tobacco's pocket", "he's oil", "insurance", "timber", "she's nuclear", "pharmaceuticals", and others? But is it not also known that an occasional departure from the principal interest may be used to show smidgindependence? And make available your palm for the balm of green? Aye, there's the rub. For lobbyists would like to own you, but you should remain steadfast in your devotion to living the life of a rental.

Never sell your political soul. Rent it!

Thou canst then lift up thy eyes unto the final mark-up in committee from whence cometh your hope and your joy. Seize the moment in the mark-up when the issue hangs in the balance. Then should you lift up thy calloused palms for rental solace and consolation amongst your colleagues who also rent rather than sell.

Then turn to the apathetic goats of the fields and the sheep of the pastures, and say to them in loud and resonant intonations, "I have kept the faith: I have not sold out to the special interests."

Chapter 5:

MONEYVANGELISTS ARE BORN OF PROFITSY

Now it was known throughout the land that religious evangelists didst personally deliver their messages of love and charity throughout the world. Didst they not travel to all corners of the earth? Didst they not bear the brutal extremes of weather, the loneliness of distant travel, the discomfort of poor lodgings, and the scarcity of the amenities of life? Didst they and their families not sacrifice for the benefit of those they served?

But Behold! There slithered forth from the grasses a host of imitators who wouldst sing, say, and do whatsoever was necessary to prosper mightily.

They kneweth not the brutal extremes of weather, but they came to know the warmth of studio platforms.

They kneweth not the loneliness and discomfort of distant travel, but they came to know first-class travel and luxurious suites in many-starred abodes. And they didst know the many weaknesses and vulnerabilities of the people.

They became crafty hucksters who kneweth the ways of the carnival of life.

And they suckered forth and grasped the hard-earned treasure of the heavy-burdened, the sad of heart, the poor of spirit, and the weak of body.

Lo! They became <u>moneyvangelists</u>! Now, as moneyvangelists became a growth industry, some moneyvangelists developed their own trademark hair style or helmet-like wigs; some came to wear flowing robes of spendor; some wore rings of flashing stones which adorned the hand that grasped the microphone; and many prospered to have large, carpeted platforms for pacing and pitching.

It came to pass that many moneyvangelists slithered from the grasses of their beginnings into the grass roots of Politics. And they didst slither into the center ring of Politics with great ease, for it was known that the skills of the Politician and the Moneyvangelists art the same. Thus, the moneyvangelists became Politicians in ministers' clothing, and they couldst change their cloth and their cloak as the moment required.

And they proclaimed their role as protectors against the liberal media. They prospered in accordance with their ability to whinalize, beg, and thunderate fearsome images of the next life of those who giveth not of their treasure. And the multitudes have given mightily.

And the moneyvangelists lustily huckstered false and scurrilous political tapes in the name of religion. They selleth all manner of things, but mostly, they gaze heavenward as they directeth their begging to the people who art before them or to the cameras which art placed on the best-profile side.

They began to build their political kingdom on earth as they mastered the art of oratorical falphonics.

Now, with the passing of time and money, the moneyvangelists have prospered in accordance with their ability to motivate the multitudes to giveth of their treasure. The moneyvangelist didst urge their flocking followers to build their stately mansions in the next life, whilst giving freely that the moneyvangelists couldst build their mansions in this life.

And the moneyvangelists residuated into nonresponsive and minimal profiles whilst the liberals of their disdain brought forth improvements in civil rights, public education, health and safety, and greater protection of the soil, the sea, and the air from which all liberals, moderates, conservatives, and. . . yea, even the moneyvangelists. . . couldst survive.

Where hidest the political moneyvangelists in those days? Where were they in the cause of public education? Were they to be seen or heard fighting for the poor, for civil rights, and health? Were they struggling to protect the rights of women and the well being of children? Nay! for they were busy preparing new grovelations for more gold and power.

Now it has come to pass that the many huckstering moneyvangelists, who are Politicians in ministers' clothing, have prevailed over the quiet and sincere leaders of the neighborhood churches, synagogues, and mosques that serveth the people who abide about them.

Thus was fulfilled the profitsy that the moneyvangelists shouldst prosper throughout the land.

And in these days, they continue to change their cloth and their cloak as the political moment may require. They form political coalitions to gain the power to impose their special creeds upon others; they expandeth their power by enlisting those who prefer the ease of followship to the effort of thinking; and they continue to thunderate with arroganatual certainty as they thrust forth their itchy palms.

Now it behooveth all politicians to learn the ways of the moneyvangelists who art now politicians in the robes of religion. For has it not come to pass that moneyvangelists have risen to great fiscal heights in accordance with their ability to motivate the multitudes to give of their treasure? Has it not also been said that treasure canst corrupt as well as rust but, being of the pacing platforms, have they found their way to fiscal salvation? Have not the moneyvangelists sold tapes, high-resonance books, and other political propaganda materials whilst they pay no taxes?

Learn thee, therefore, from these brethren and sistren of the open palms, and then shall thou likewise find new ways of filling thy treasure boxes to overflowing. Transpalmed cash may be well for thee as politicians, but removing the trans from the palms giveth palms with fulsome taking but no giving. Verily, it canst give thee more intake without the risks of being caught.

Chapter 6:

LAMENTATIONS, PRAYERS AND PSALMS

O Powers-That-Be, Give us Courage

O Powers-That-Be, keep our minds from wandering along the pathways of truth wherein defeat may be nurtured.

For thou knowest that truth may reveal our grasp for gold, our lust for power, and our fear of an aroused populace which mayeth evolve from the revelations of truth.

Help, O Powers-That-Be, to keep our hearts from softening to the pleas of those who suffer injustice from those whom we appoint to do our bidding;

For thou knoweth that sustained political strength cometh from unseeing eyes, from unhearing ears, and from uncaring hearts. Is not pragmatism the idol of all political leaders even though its worship tarnisheth the golden dreams of a society? Is not the hard nose developed to reign to over the soft heart?

Therefore, O Powers-That-Be, give us the strength, the courage, the hardened heart, the grasping greed, and the lust for power that shall sustain us as we abide in the marble halls of public service.

O Powers-That-Be, save us from the incursions of fresh and unsettling ideas. These are perilous times, for transplamations of cash and other treasure now cometh with greater danger of disclosure. We ask for thy guidance and help. Is the time at hand when the mother cow hath given its all?

O Powers-That-Be, let not the mother cow collapse, for much depends on her. But if the mother cow collapseth, let her collapse not in our pastures, but in the pastures of our enemies. Then canst we as colleagial protectors run and buck with the goats of the hills. Let us bleat with the sheep of the pastures; let us wail with the toilers of the fields. For if we run, buck, bleat, and wail with skill and sincerity of demeanor, we may continue to lead.

Give us courage, O Powers-That-Be. When the sounds of war art fanned by defense contractors and media pundits, give us the courage to find those who wouldst take up our own intrigue, fight our fights, and die our deaths.

For verily, then shall we stand humbly by their still sides to listen reverently to bugles sounding taps. With fervent patriotism, shall we pay tribute to them on national holidays; our oratory shall thunder mightily with roundness of vowels; and we shall wave hundreds and hundreds of flags at scores and scores of parades.

With bold words and majestic gestures, we shall praise their courage and devotion to duty as they paid the supreme sacrifice to preserve our property and our way of life. Of such will be our courage, O Powers-That-Be, that we will praise ye who buildeth the machines of war . . . and who buildeth them with hidden billing fraudulence and optimal enflagations. For we knoweth, O Powers-That-Be, that if ye hadst not meant for us to wage war, ye wouldst not have given us guns and other weapons of mass destruction.

Through sharing such courage, we canst survive to fight the good fight again and again. Surely, the sacrifices of our forefathers and foremothers deserve no less!

A Politician's Prayer

O Powers-That-Be, deliver us, the Politicians of the world, from the knowledge of the people. Keepeth them in satisfied ignorance that they shalt remain as contented as the goats in the fields and the sheep in the pastures.

Let them knoweth not our ways; hideth from them the vacuuity of our minds, the arrogance of our souls, and the mushiness of our hearts.

Save us from the people's knowledge of our selective devotion to issues and from the potential regret of their own apathy. For 'tis more acceptable that representative government be destroyed slowly by the oozing pollutal sludge of apathetic ignorance than by the shattering jolt of sudden, but too-late, discovery. Sludge may ooze with peace, whereas jolts may reveal through hesitant conflict.

Therefore, O Powers-That-Be, jolteth not the people into the light of early discovery. Let the wool remaineth over their eyes and grant us our continuing leadership in the Kingdom of Blathering Goats and Bleating Sheep.

Psalm of Faithfulness

If I forget thee, O Powers-That-Be, let my tongue cleave to the roof of my mouth that my mumbles shall be weak in their intonalities.

If I turn my back on thee, O Powers-That-Be, let my head be vulnerable to the jawbone of an ass, and let my spine tremble in the fear of the unknown that surely shall come to pass.

HOWEVER, if I sing not thy praises when I sing to the goats in the fields and the sheep in the pastures, know ye that public rebukes mean not that I forget ye, or

that I turneth my back on ye; for public rebukes pre-
serveth my place in the office where in I shall serve ye.

Knowest that regardless of my public words,
always shall I remember thee in the private halls of public
power. Thy will shall be done; and of thy treasure, a
widow's mite shall be mine.

A Psalm of Creative Memories

O Powers-That-Be, Blessed art those whose memories art flexible and creative, whose profound perplexity
canst be assuringly contained.

Blessed art the voters whose memories of my
promises shalt fade with kindness, whose memories of my
firm handshake and broad smile shalt be fixed with a permanent and positive recall.

Blessed are the defense contractors, their flacks,
and the flacks' flacks in the media, for verily they shall be
my friend forever as they spin their messages for fiscal
squeeze.

Blessed art those who forgetteth the magnitude of
my lies and the extent of my illegal actions as I furrow my
brow with creative sincerity, waveth the flag and speaketh
of family values.

Blessed art the huckstering moneyvangelists and
their political coalition whose quest for gold and power
doth make us spiritual partners.

Blessed art the givers of cash whose supply canst
match their enthusiasm even as I stroke their egos and fulfill their greedistic desires.

Blessed art the gullible in mind, the joyful in spirit,
and the selfish in heart.

For they art the foundation of the greedocracy
which I shalt serve to the end of my political days.

147

The Citizens' Psalm

Help me, O People-Who-Care, for the waters are cometh to my neck and they are waters fully polluted from the chemicals of the fields, the litter of the highways, the garbage of the cities, the acids of the rains, the toxins of industries, the wastes of nuclear churns, the soils of the barnyards, and the political enrichments of Washington, London, Ottawa, Moscow, Tokyo, Tel Aviv, Brazilia and other centers of politicians.

I sink in deep mire, where there is no bottom: I come unto substances where the gasses of the air overcometh me even as I gasp for one last syllable of elusive truth.

I am weary of my crying: my thoat is dry; my muscles acheth: my mind grapples for meaning; and mine eyes fail while I search for a purposeful path.

They that fooleth me with no other cause than political power are more than the hairs which falleth from my head.

O People-Who-Care, thou knowest my love of democracy; thou knowest the tears which floweth from mine eyes like a mighty river when I seeist the pillars of democracy crumble one after another to the poisons of ethnic hatred, racial bigotry, religious wars, the greed of politicians, and the moral bankruptcy of our leaders.

Is it not true that those who art not purchasable for gold fall by the wayside of public service? When. . . Oh when, I pleadingly ask, will the Mount Hokum of Apathy which supporteth the pillars of greed be swept away by the power of The-People-Who-Care? I pray that I, or my spirit, may be a part of the great sweep.

Chapter 7:

APATHESIUM

Knowest ye goats of the hills, ye sheep of the pastures, and ye toilers of the fields, that the leaders of opposing political groups breaketh bread together, drinketh wine together, and divideth the spoils one with the other according to their numbers, their negotiation skills and their pecking order.

The breaking, drinking and dividing being done in the darkened rooms away from the view of the people giveth rise to greater appetites among the political leaders, their bag carriers and their toadies. And the great appetites increaseth like unto the weeds, the ticks of the woods, and the vipers of the marble halls.

But, verily, even as ye learneth but liketh not the ways of the politicians, there are millions among ye who careth not.

Canst those who careth not be inspired to care enough to challenge the politicians whose greed for gold and lust for power art destroying the life of our representative republic?

Or, wilt the careth-nots multiply in numbers and influence until the political system gluggles downward into the sewers of Despotism in a final swirling and tonal tribute to Apathy?

What thinketh ye? How carest ye?

PART FOUR:

*Tranquil Reflections for
Career Enrichment*

Every successful politician or bureaucrat occasionally escapes the turmoil of the daily routine to ponder the marginal verities of life.

Such escapes may be a short stroll along a path of some lobbyist's hideaway; it may be a residuation on a park bench while waiting for a friendly bag man; it may be on a non-lurching flight to some interest group's conference; or it may be a comfortable chair in one's own home.

Whatever form the escape may be, it may provide a few minutes for reflective thought . . . an open mind and an open palm. Let these be free-floating thoughts that swirl about you in a bubblistic orgy of creativity. Some of them may enrich your political career.

These marginal verities are shared with you in the hope they will be helpful and inspirational as you wander along the path of happy politics.

Malpractice Insurance for Politicians

Malpractice insurance has been used primarily for the protection of doctors and hospitals . . . protection against real or trumped-up suits.

But what about the poor old malpracticing politician? His malpractice deals with bribes, kickbacks, payroll fraud, or other forms of stealing.

How would malpractice insurance pay off for the politician who is caught with his hand in the cookie jar? He would not be paid off in money, because he would have already stashed his cash.

To a politician, there is no greater calamity than to be zilchified into disgrace and to have no more power than the average lowly taxpayer or non-voting citizen. The pay-off? The politicians would be provided homes in

Malpractice City . . . a city that would be inhabited only
by fallen politicians and a few of their hacks and flacks.

Malpractice City would have its own lake for laun-
dering dirty money, . . . its own bank for numbered
accounts . . . its own radio and television studios for in-
house speeches and loud harangues. What about a news-
paper for those who love printer's ink - The Flat Earth
Daily Bugle?

To accommodate the different tastes for the politicians, the city planners could build various housing areas...
such as Kickback Woods, Under-the-Table Pines, Plain-
Envelope Estates, or . . . Greased Palm Ridge.

Of course, malpractice insurance won't become a
reality until the members of Congress can find a way to
make the taxpayers pay for the premiums. Think about it.
If you bubble upward to the highest levels of politics, you
may be able to perfect the concept of Malpractice
Insurance for Politicians. What a legacy you can leave for
generations of other malpracticers!

Loophole Golf

One of the most common but unpublicized games
played in Washington is "Loophole Golf". It's a friendly
little game played between a lobbyist and a member of
Congress. Out on the golf course, there are no telephone
calls or beeping pagers. And there are no other lobbyists
to compete for the attention of the member of Congress.

How do you score Loophole Golf? At the end of
the 18th hole, before going to the 19th hole, the players
measure the size and shape of the loophole, AND they
count the number of strokes on the palm of the politician.

By the way, one major defense contractor gained

such snuggling privileges with members of the Armed Services Committee that it was able to obtain $418,000 of your tax money to pay for the maintenance and operations of its company park. And the executives of that company received more than $20,000 worth of golf balls at taxpayers' expense. Of course, this is nothing compared to the millions of dollars involved in Loophole Golf.

Yes, the old pirates of the high seas could never match the public plunder taken by today's Pirates of the Potomac . . . pirates who have traded swords and blunderbuses for bags of golf clubs . . . pirates who have learned to play the easier, safer, and more profitable game of loophole golf. Learn to play the game. Find a desperate but friendly lobbyist to show you around an easy course, and you will thrive with the green from the greens.

The Steering Wheel

Have you ever pondered the unusual power of a steering wheel? While sitting under my favorite old oak tree smoking my pipe, my thoughts orbitated around the tremendous transformation in the personalities of people when they are behind the steering wheel of a car.

A quiet, decent lady can become a vocal hoot owl when some thoughtless driver forces his or her way in front of her on the road, at an intersection, or in a shopping mall's parking lot. Similarly, a very decent and polite gentleman can be transformed into a Rambo tank driver when confronted by a traffic jam, gridlock, or an extremely slow driver in a no-passing zone. The steering wheel is gripped with white-knuckled anger and a facial grimace. A loud mumble may be followed by some violence-oriented snort or resonating roar. I think the steering wheel may be the transforming instrument.

Now, if the steering wheel is a transforming instrument that converts reasonable and decent people into angry and aggressive individuals, perhaps there are some constructive uses for this motivational power. Can we use the steering wheel as a training tool for the members of the armed forces? When new recruits arrive at a base for

basic training, should they be issued steering wheels along with their backpacks and rifles? Should our men in uniform being sent into battle be given disposable steering wheels to hold in their hands for a few minutes before being given the order to charge? Would holding such a disposable steering wheel in their hands for a few minutes stimulate the adrenal glands, stir the flow of blood, and build an angry spirit to fight?

Just as the steering wheel brings an immediate change in the personality of a person who grips one, so also is there a change in the personality of a citizen when gripping the hand of a candidate for public office. An other-

wise reasonable, decent American can become a snarling, insulting interrogator when confronting a candidate.
Having been a candidate for high public office, I met many wonderful people and made many new friends, but I also met people who were transformed from friendly pussycats into snarling tigers when they learned I was a candidate.

Is there a relationship between steering wheels and candidates? Can steering wheels and defeated candidates be useful to the nation in times of great crisis? Perhaps this may be worthy of study by a Presidential Task Force. . . or, at least a Blue Ribbon Commission. Think of it! A Presidential Task Force on Steering Wheel Aggression. Or, Steering Wheels for National Defense. If you should ever be defeated, you may refine the idea into a legislative proposal for some friend to introduce. It can be a nice consolation prize.

If the proposal runs into strong opposition from the person who defeated you, don't fight it. Simply quietly arrange for the concept to be included as an add-on to some defense contract. Contractors can always make use of your contacts. In the Valley of the Potomac, happiness is a scratched back.

The Rumperatory Featherheads

Have you ever wondered why many politicians are often referred to as "birdbrains," "turkeys," "featherheads," "buzzards," and other types of birds?

My research into the question deals primarily with two general categories.

First are the breeding birds. . . the most common... about 650 different species that nest regularly in North America. Their breeding and nesting areas are to be

found in Washington, Ottawa, Mexico and in all state or
provincial captitals. A few sightings have been reported
in local jurisdictions.

A second category of political birds include the regular Washington visitors. . . those birds which migrate to
the Valley of the Potomac in search of non-repayable loans
or large quantities of military equipment. Some of the regular visitors are Presidents, Prime Ministers, Kings, military officers and others whose warm embraces of friendship are concluded with the salute of an outstretched palm.
Gold braid, stars and medals always excite the Washington
breeding birds in the Pentagon or on Capitol Hill.

So try your hand at political birdwatching. Get out
your binoculars. Observe the nocturnal coots, squawkers,
fiscal skimmers, sleazy twirpheads, rumperatory tingle-
coots, and many variables of vultures and boardroom
thrashers. Check their breeding patterns.

The political breeding birds rarely have sex with
one another. What they do, they do to the host country's
taxpayers.

Blessed be the Tape that Binds

As the President of the International Association of
Professional Bureaucrats, I know all about red tape. The
politicians and bureaucrats of the world are not opposed to
cutting red tape. . . as long as it is cut lengthwise! This, of
course, produces more red tape.

Any day now, I expect a special report from NASA
that one of our space probes has found that our earth is
being converted into a large mass of red tape. It may be a
major factor in global warming. Think about it. . . An
astronaut in space turns his camera towards our planet and

157

sends back pictures of the earth wrapped in pulsating red tape. A great throbbing mass. Some of the loose ends of tape whipping around like long, red boa constrictors... trying to find another place in which to bite, choke and hold. And our great globe may begin to tilt a little more... and the earth's rotation on its axis may become slower and slower. Could it come to a loud, squeaking, grinding halt? What a nightmare! Ughhhhhhhhhh! The Red Tape that binds the universe into a single writhing blob!

Monuments for Bureaucrats

Wherever I have traveled around the world, I have seen many statues and monuments. Most of them are tributes to military heroes or to perceived political leaders. Occasionally, I have seen a statue of a musician, a poet, or a great teacher, but it is the military hero who seems to prevail in the great mountains of bronze profiles.

Military heroes? Well, many of the statues of the military are of genuine heroes, but sometimes the statues may be of hometown boys who muddled it to the rank of colonel or general while not really performing any acts of heroism. Maybe they rose to that rank by knowing how to play the military bureaucracy. There's nothing wrong with that, and perhaps some towns have a difficult time in coming up with something or someone to be proud of. Of course, there are many real heroes who are never cast in bronze.

Capital cities seem to have more statues per capita than all other cities of the world. Washington, D.C. certainly has its share. It requires a professional guide to identify the people honored in bronze, and one often wonders who made the decisions on those honored and not honored. In both Washington and New York, it is common to observe people standing at the feet of a bronzed hero, not so much in admiration of the subject of the statue, but to feed the swirling pigeons that have their own way of paying respect to the bronzed hero.

There is one category of statue I have never seen, and it is a category of many unsung but worthy heroes. The federal and state bureaucrats! They are the ones who keep the government going from day to day. With all the marginal thinking and pompistrutting which goes on in the Congress and in the top levels of the Executive Branch, just doing one's job is not all that easy.

About the time some middle level government employee is about to complete some assignment, he or she may be interrupted by "a Congressional" . . . a letter with a printed buckslip bearing a rubber-stamped signature of a member of Congress. The processing of these top priority letters is so time consuming, the bureaucrat has difficulty doing the principal task he or she was hired to do. This type of daily interruption does not lead to identified hero-ism, but its institutional or combined effect is the essence of the daily battle the working bureaucrats must fight.

Another type of bureaucratic performance that leads to heroism is the work of a competent whistle-blow-er who is a peoples' watchdog wanting to see that the tax-payers get a dollar value for a dollar spent. Or, perhaps wants to halt sloppy, haphazard, politically influenced operations that may involve a type of fraud. A whistle-blower striving to preserve the integrity of a governmental system is a hero.

Then there is the government bureaucrat who steps into the gap when superiors may be snared, mangled and mired in the muck of a scandal. This type of bureaucrat keeps the wheels of government functioning. . . or who mans the Ship of State. The U.S. federal government almost came to a standstill during the Watergate era, and several offices were mired during the "arms for hostages" fiasco know as Irangate. Zippergate, which was a partisan-media fixation, also had some negative effect in the performance levels of various offices. Heroes? Those who continued to do their real jobs.

My point? It behooves you as a politician to support an appropriation for a few million for statues or monuments to the faceless, hardworking, and competent bureaucrats who have plugged along daily in behalf of the taxpayer. It would be a wise political step and it might encourage the present corps of bureaucrats to provide cover for you and your colleagues.

Halljogging

People like to think of public servants as hard working, competent, and powerful officials who are representing them effectively in the halls of power. Politicians and bureaucrats have an obligation to present that image to the public, for it contributes to a tranquil and peaceful reality. One of the image-enhancing skills which can be mastered with great ease is that of halljogging.

The discovery of halljogging was made when I returned to the United States after working in Latin America in the foreign service. I realized that I had only a short period of time in which to establish the reputation I wanted in the new headquarters environment. My assignment was one which I had orbitated into existence myself, and few colleagues really understood what it was. This made the matter of image-in-a-short-time even more important.

I began using the standard techniques around executive offices. I initiated telephone calls during the lunch hour; this assured that my telephone would be ringing much of the afternoon. I made a number of requests for material from friends on Capitol Hill; this guaranteed a flow of important "Congressional" mail. I ordered various bulletins and catalogs from other agencies and private businesses; this not only assured a flow of mail but it also established my self-selected title and my own mail address in the mail room. After a short time, the telephone book for the State Department included my office with my title and address. Then it was time to *halljog*.

Once every morning and once every afternoon, sometimes twice in the afternoon, I would halljog. That

is, I would stride around all the halls, on every floor, carrying a file folder under my arm. I would place a file folder high up under my arm and carry it as a football player would carry a football. With a forward tilt of my body, and a furrowed brow, I would move as rapidly as I could around the building. The folder was always high under my arm. Never did I carry the file folder at my side; that indicated my mission was not very important. Absolutely never did I halljog with a briefcase. A briefcase would have projected the wrong image. . . arriving late or leaving early. Occasionally, someone would try to stop me for conversation. My response: "Sorry I can't talk with you right now. I'll call you when I get back to my office." Then I would return to my office and have a cup of coffee.

Within a matter of weeks, people began to talk about me. I was identified as a competent and very busy man. Working on something important. To enhance the image even more, I would use the same technique when going from one building to another. . . or going "downtown" in the agencies or on Capitol Hill. Always with a file folder high under my arm, with a forward tilt, and a carefully cultivated furrowed brow, and I would halljog as rapidly as a shortlegged fat man could jog. Halljogging. An excellent image enhancement technique that works! Try it. You'll like it.

St. Basil, Curly, Larry and Moe

St. Basil, the godfather of modern astrology in Oklahoma, put aside his crossword puzzle to share with me his interpretation of cosmic forces and their influence on matters of the environment. A former university president, St. Basil became the guru of modern astrology, and as such gave much advice to political leaders, business executives, con artists and others. Though he occasionally consulted the stars and other heavenly bodies, he usually preferred to shuffle cards and dominoes before making his weighty pronouncements. When he spoke, it was to break long periods of prodigious pondering, and he spoke in deep tones and with powerful words.

On one of my last visits with him, I sought an explanation of governmental and moonal influences on the rivers and lakes of Northeastern Oklahoma. . . particularly the officially designated scenic Illinois River. I asked,

"Why do the people who profess to love the Illinois pollute
it with random abandon? Why do the people who make
great profits by renting canoes and recreation facilities
along the river refuse to work actively to protect it from
pollution?" He nodded his head in a nod of understanding,
then signaled for more questions. "Why do the chicken
factory operators do the least they can to obey the pollution
laws which are on the books? Why are the hog factories
that produce so many tons of hog waste and stinking odors
that cover the countryside run by people who don't care?
More important, why do some of the politicians of the area
represent the chicken poopers and hog manurers more than
they represent the people who elect them?"

The room was silent. Then he pursed his lips,
slowly nodded his head in understanding, and shifted his
position in his large leather chair. He gazed at the dominoes before him until his eyes seemed to betray a trance-
like study of one of the great mysteries of Green Country,
Oklahoma. His red hair falteringly flowed over his fore-
head, and he slowly raised his right hand to point to the
firmament of the heavens. Then sounds filled the room
with rolls of thunder as he spoke.

"The forces of Pluto and Venus are orbitating for a
residuating level of neanderthalic influence. The p e o p l e
and p o l i t i c i a n s are squattling!" He dragged out the
words "people and politicians". He squinted with his right
eye, drew a circle in the air with his finger, and grunted, a
single, "Harrrrrrummmph." It was belly-shaking, diaphramic grunt. Having made his pronouncement, he then folded
his arms, and continued to gaze at the dominoes.

"But tell me, St. Basil, what does this mean?
When people and politicians squattle, what do they do?"

He turned his head in my direction; he raised his

eyebrows in disbelief. I did not know the process of squattling. "They are sitting it out until the problem goes away."

"That doesn't make much sense," I said. "Every
day more and more lakes are becoming dead lakes where
people can't swim, can't fish, or scuba dive. And can't take
a breath of unpolluted air. And yet, the people and politicians squattle?"

St. Basil squinted again, checked his charts, then
jabbed the air with his finger. "Yessss." He smiled out of
one side of his mouth, "They say they are waiting for all
the evidence to come in. And they want more no-future
minimum wage jobs. The Big Three. . . Curly, Larry, and
Moe. . . Boren, don't you get it? They speak the language
of caring, but their thumbs-down gestures before the legislative committees and their introductions of the polluters
around the legislative halls speak the real message of their
political purpose."

Then came the gestalt. The configuration. The
parts came together. Curly, Larry and Moe!

St. Basil started to shuffle his dominoes. "Do you
want me to cast another horoscope to explain it?"

"No, I understand now," I said. "And I'll remember." How could I have been so dumb to forget? All that's
stupid does not fail. The history of legislation proves it.
People who want clean air, soil, and water are the easiest
marks for established politicians to con.

The New Productivity: Hushput-Mushput-Flushput

For the early years in the development of industrial
America, the standard approach to measuring productivity
was by evaluating the input and output of an organizational unit. More accurately, it was the input-thruput-output

method, with the thruput being the stage or process between the beginning and the end. Though the input-output factors are usually recognized as the basic standards, the often ignored element of thruput is important, because it measures the time required to produce whatever is being produced. The timality stretch or shrinkage obviously influences the bottom line of productivity.

As the role of image became increasingly important to any enterprise. . . particularly in evaluating such factors as leadership, corporate managerial practices, and political performance, it also became important in assessing all endeavors, public and private. The image of performance is easier to understand than performance itself; it is also safer to achieve. If a person does something, he or she may make a mistake; if a person can acquire the image of performance, however, the advantages of performance will be gained without the accompanying risks that attend actual performance itself. The measurement of image is mushified by the linguistic adjustivity the public accepts in the appraisal of performance.

The assessment of productivity, therefore, shifted from input-thruput-output to hushput-mushput-flushput in which the hushput is the approximate input, mushput is the meandering trail of processing, and flushput is the irretrievable filing of final product estimates. This new productive assessment can work extremely well for many years but ultimately the conclusion can be catastrophic. A business enterprise can collapse, an academic institution can flounder, and a politician can lose an election. Only religious institutions can continue to depend heavily on the hushput-mushput-flushput formula, because the vital element of faith is difficult for pre-death evaluation.

What does it all mean? God only knows.

Twiggles, Molarchecks, Boobidoodles and Thinkidoodles

Staying awake is not always an easy thing to do, yet the ability to withstand the blows of mind-muddling bags of mush is important at high levels of corporate, political, or religious life. Lack of sleep at night, heavy eating and perhaps a glass of wine to top it off, and being in a dark, stuffy, meeting room with monotonal non-messages floating in the air are enough to induce a droopy-eyed, head-nodding pattern of behavior.

Boring meetings such as political dinners, trade association sessions, faculty meetings, committee conferences, and cacotonal sermons are particular challenges. Monotonal, minimal or smothered thoughts are not stimulating to either the mind or the body. How, then, can one stay awake when every reasonable message to the brain suggests that a nice nap may be in order?

In my personal experience, I have developed four techniques that have been particularly helpful to me: (1) twiggling, (2) molarchecking, (3) boobidoodling, and (4) thinkidoodling.

Twiggling involves wiggling one's toes in various patters. For example, the twiggler can alternately wiggle the toes of the left foot and the right foot in a simple patter of 1,2,1,2,1,2. Or the toes of one foot can be wiggled five times, and the toes of the other foot can then be wiggled one time or up to whatever number of times may be interesting. In long meetings, one can even keep count of the numbers-per-minute of twiggles performed in various patterns. Twiggling should be fun as well as useful. One precaution, however: never twiggle so vigorously that an observer can see the top of your shoes moving. That may reveal you're not paying attention.

Molarchecking, another avenue for creative escape from public dozing, is executed by counting one's teeth with the tongue. It permits the molarcheckor to appear to be attentive while actually staring somewhat vacantly at the speaker or chairperson of the meeting. Like twiggling, molarchecking can be done using various patterns. One can count the uppers. . . beginning between the two eyeteeth and moving to the left and then from the middle to the right. Full sweep molarchecking from one side to the other can be used as a diversion. The lowers can be counted in a similar manner. Individual styles can emerge as practice and experience with various styles make molarchecking more comfortable as a stay-awake mechanism.

While twiggling and molarchecking are techniques which can be used regardless of the meeting environment, *boobidoodling* and *thinkidoodling* require a table or an arrangement where note-taking is appropriate. A boobidoodle is a particular type of doodle which is inspired by the proceedings or the marginal thoughts being presented by the speaker. It is not based on the boobiness of the

BOOBIDOODLE

A specialized type of non-sensical doodle. Boobidoodles are drawn by boobidoodlators during boring staff meetings, professional or technical conferences, and committee meetings. Boobidoodles usually reflect the boobiness of the presentations made at the meeting and not the boobiness of the boobidoodlator.

person doing the doodle but primarily on the boobiness of what is being presented. As an artistic type of nonsensical doodle, boobidoodles are formed in all shapes and sizes. They can combine straight lines with angles or curves along with inclusionary or exclusionary circles or arcs. In short, boobidoodles are exciting enough by the essence of boobiness that they serve very well as stay-awake vehicles.

Thinkidoodles, on the other hand, are a type of doodle drawn while a person is actually thinking. It is, therefore, a focused and constructive doodle which, when preserved in personal files, can be used to reconstruct the thoughts at the time they were be doodled. Thinkidoodles are a graphic crutch that enables a person to survive the mental fog of a boring meeting and emerge with a useful idea. Words, shorthand notalities, and personal codes are common to all thinkidoodles.

Boobidoodles are survival-oriented. Thinkidoodles are idea-oriented and are, therefore, quite rare. If you are a member of a committee and wish merely to stay awake, become a boobidoodlator. If, on the other hand, you have some problem to solve or some speech to outline, you may wish to thinkidoodle your way through the meeting. You can translate your thinkidoodles into meaningful notes at a later time.

A National Insect

The Bald Eagle is our national bird, and the rose is our national flower. Now, I like the Bald Eagle . . . and I have enjoyed seeing them as I have walked the back-coun-try trails of the United States and Canada as well as watching them near my home in the foothills of the Ozarks. I also like roses, and I enjoy giving them to my lovely wife, Norma. There is another national identity that needs to be filled: a national insect.

Of all the animal species in the world, five of every six are insects. Scientists have described nearly one million different species of insects, and entomologists estimate there are from one to four million species yet to be described and classified.

Some insects are so small they are barely visible, and some are several inches long. Some live for only a few hours, and some live for many years. Fossils indicate that primitive insects developed some 350 million years ago.

So which one should we select as our national insect? As we consider a few of the possibilities, think of how each could reflect the reality and image of our nation.

Butterflies - beautiful, majestic, and nondirectional in its flight.

Gnats - fearless little critters which can go eye-to-eye and nose-to-nose with anyone.

Fleas - high-jumping warriors whose biting attacks can move Kings, Presidents, and even bureaucrats to action.

Lice - moving inspirers which can motivate stupid people to scratch their heads and cause political half-wits to nit their wits . . . creating the image of a thoughtful people.

Cockroaches - The wily and leggy creatures that cross-fertilize the filth of dumps with the kitchens of the fastidious. Equalizing survivors!

Ticks - From pinhead size to large skin-burrowing varieties, they give us meaning for our political life . . . poly, meaning many, and ticks, for bloodsuckers.

And on and on... Think of the possibilities! A national insect for national identity! Think of the good that insects do. They promote the decay of organic material, and they help in the formation of soil. They pollinate many plants, and they are a major part of our food chain. They add beauty and they play a major role in the balance of Nature.

Now, other than pollination, that's more than most members of Congress can do. Perhaps we need a Committee for the Selection of a National Insect.

Guidelines for Meeting Planners

In most organizations, the most important but most frequently under-rated member of the team is the person who is responsible for planning and organizing meetings. I have known many outstanding meeting planners. . . most notably with IBM, but I have never met one who was not competent and diligent in making a meeting an effective event in support of their organization's purpose. In politics, competent meeting planners are vital to successful campaigns.

Over the years, I have doodled a number of flow charts for meeting planners, and I have succeeded fairly well in all types of sessions other than political meetings, where the purpose is the transpalmation of cash. My role was as a professional humorist on the platform, not as a professional planner. Nevertheless, the osmotic processes of learning came into play, and after speaking at more than two thousand major meetings, I think I understand the process quite well. There is no single chart or organogram, as they are called in Brazil, that will meet every organization's needs, but the most common involve an ebb and flow of variable factors that orbitate within the parameters of full achievement. The decisionary flow chart and the guidelines which I am happy to share with my friends and other possible readers are basic in most planning sessions.

170

The Planning Guidelines

1. Follow the ebb and flow of the Decisionary Flow Chart.
2. To control the planning, maneuver for the selection of Conference Co-chairs who are not close together either geographically or philosophically. Keep the discussions on the big picture, and you will be able to do what you want by the way you handle the details.
3. Select an understandable theme, but fuzzify the objectives to guarantee flexibility of the meeting evaluation. Fuzzified goals are always met; clear and precise goals do not leave maneuvering room.
4. Encourage innovation in the planning session. . . but keep the innovation within established guidelines.
5. Globate all meeting issues. By globating or looking at the big picture, you can never be backed into a corner.
6. Refer problems to a committee. If you study a problem long enough, it may go away. Nothing is impossible until it is sent to a committee.
7. Develop a sound program of public hype and media flackification. Image is more important than performance.
8. Profundify simplicity. If people understand what is going on, they may want to take control.
9. Trashify all reports with irrelevant data, maps, charts, and computer readouts.
10. Bury the minutes of previous meetings. Boren Advisory: Forgetting the right things is better than remembering the wrong things.
11. Give most of your attention to the concluding part of the meeting. Be sure that participants leave the meeting with a warm glow of friendship, a sense of satisfaction, and a feeling of real or imagined accomplishment.
12. If things go wrong in spite of your best planning, residuate into a low profile, hunkerfy into a psychological crouch, and sit it out until you know which way to jump. Potentis reposit obscurantum. (In obscurity lies strength.)
13. Finally, follow another Boren Advisory: If you want to control the outcome of a meeting, don't preside; write the minutes.

(If you think the number 13 is unlucky, you shouldn't plan a meeting.)

Boren's Political Guide to Washington

At a coffee session with political supporters, at a special interest conference, or when confering with your subordinates, you can project the image of being a well-informed authority on Washington and world events without being encumbered with knowledge itself. Merely select randomly (from top to bottom) a phrase from each group of wordalities. With practice you can fuzzify any concept at the drop of a memo!

Group 1

a. Based on the skills in rearranging the truth into believable lies,
b. Within the abstructions of the Fed concerning future changes in interest rates,
c. Disregarding the economic sniffles and the Post-Nafta Drift,
d. To harmonize the rules on applied ignorance,
e. While fuzzy guidelines must be in accord with new bipartisan strategies,
f. In developing a subset of politically interdigitated sequencing skills,
g. Now that the warm weather will bring a record crop of ticks,
h. Recognizing the excessive flood of untreated political sewage,
i. While the transpalming of cash still reigns as the essence of a meaningful handshake,
j. Considering the pressure to reduce taxes,

Group 2

a. the proficiency-based streams of criterion references
b. the PACal flow of cash or other trading assets
c. all the relevant factors within the circle of creative decisions
d. any group of lobbyists skilled in the game of loophole golf
e. the long range effects of the fast track factors
f. the most notable currency trades
g. the conference committee report
h. ready access to the White House
i. the responsiveness of the media to hypal control by the White House
j. Congressional idiotoxicities which will become evident to all who read the newspapers

Group 3

a. will increase the outstretched palms of most Washington lawyers,

b. may cause an increase in the bloatational floatum in the legislative processes,

c. should elevate the rhetorical integrity of political debate,

d. may translateralize the cash and other non-traceable pay-offs,

e. shall darken the prospects for meaningful modalities in the next election,

f. may reduce the impact of integrity-oriented policies,

g. should engoosate the political approach to target servicing,

h. can help in the bladderation of committee meetings,

i. can implement a program of issue dispersality,

j. could be reflected in the boobidoodles of White House staffers,

Group 4

a. because ignorance has never reduced the level of debate in Congress.

b. provided the voters never discover the pork-barrel imperatives in legislative deals.

c. unless the Pentagon and the defense contractors are in a compassionate mood.

d. insofar as it is not known by the taxpayers.

e. even when the media representatives play the game their bosses want played.

f. unless there is agreement among those administering the appropriate laws and regulations.

g. as long as they are within the snortations of huckerstering political moneyvangelists.

h. unless the cross-cultural linkages are absquatulated by executive orders.

i. although the deregulation of the military rules of order may cause some discomfort.

j. even though foreign junkets are affected by the growth of terrorism in the nice places to visit.

For more marginal pearls of wisdom, check: **www.jimboren.com**

PART FIVE.

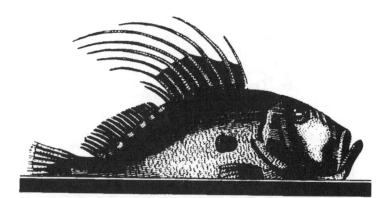

THE DICTIONARY OF BORENWORDS

-A-

abstruct (ab-struct) v. To destroy an idea, policy, or concept by making it so abstract that no one, including the abstructor, can understand what is being abstructed. Combining a combination of abstruction and abstraction, the word is particularly useful to attorneys, drafters of regulations, theater critics, members of the clergy, and politicians at all levels. Abstruct, first used in Washington in 1972, is the conceptual pioneer of the wordalities of postmodernism, a pomo style of turn-of-the-millennium mumbling which retrofits creative ignorance within the heteromodalities of academic and pseudo-social constructs.

acabu (ak'a-boo) n. An academic bureaucrat. Most acabus tend to flock together in cafeterias where they mumble about discipline (sic), school policies on grading, teachers' salaries, innovative methods of doing the same old things with new descriptions.

academize (ak-a'-dem-eyes) -v- To smother educational institutions in a blanket of red tape, layers of paper, and petrified procedures. Though very similar to macademize, the layering of roads with long-lasting impervious materials, academize is not limited to the top-to-bottom process but is equally stimulated by bottom-to-top bubbling of academizing substances. Some teachers who wish to teach are academized by administrative rulings, legislatively mandated classroom announcements, and other non-instructional intrusions into the classroom. Some teachers enjoy academizing and they become administrators.

aclutterate (a-klut'-er-ate) v. To clutter a desk or work place in an organized manner (1) for the purpose of indicating diligent and productive activity, or (2) as an expression of personal work habits. A cluttered desk is one in which papers, file folders, documents, paper clips, computer read-outs, and other materials are randomly and haphazardly strewn about a desk. An aclutterated desk, on the other hand, is one in which papers and materials are in a recoverable and extractable state while appearing to be in a state of hopeless disarray.

adagiomental (a-da'-jee-o-men'tl) adj. Slow-minded, not from an ability standpoint but from a deliberate and planned style of thinking slowly. Individuals who are adagiomental in their thinking patterns appear to be wise and worthy of respect.

anti-snoragulant (an-tee-snore-agg'-u-lunt) n. Words or phrases that will arouse dozing members of an audience, or regain attention of those whose thought may be wandering. Threats, money-offers, and sex-oriented language tend to be anti-snoragulants.

apathetics (ap-a-thetics) -n- People who are controlled by the vacuum-oriented spirit of apathy. Apathetics are happy as long as putting greens are in good shape, beaches are open, tennis courts are available, one-arm bandits spin away their money, or a good football game and a six-pack of beer are available.

arrogantual (arro-gan'-tual) -adj- Gigantic or gargantuan arrogance.

attodawdle (at'-o-daw-dl) v. (1) To delay something by placing it in the hands of an attorney, (2) a verb expressing the practice of attorneys who postpone everything by slipshod work, lost files, inadequate notes, and the inability to recall the status of a matter for which they have responsibility. Non-attorneys must consciously attodawdle, but attorneys can attodawdle without disturbing a neuron or rippling a thought. In any organization decisions can be postponed for a minimum of six months by simply asking the General Counsel for an opinion.

-B-

backupuncture, also bacupuncture (bak'-u-punk-shur) v. To skillfully insert a sharp verbal needle or other career-cutting instrument in the back of a colleague or other competitor. Backupuncture is not to be confused with clumsily executed back-stabbing. Backupuncturists rarely leave fingerprints.

bamwordle (bam-word'hl) (1) n. A word-oriented bamboozle. (2) v. To bamboozle or ram through a project, idea, or program by word-oriented bombast. Bamwordling is an effectively drivelated style of bamboozling characterized by the undetected bombast.

birective (by-rek'-tihv) n. A divided or two-way directive. Issued by those who travel both sides of the street, speak out of both sides of their mouths, or issue non-positions in the form of a birective position.

bizzify (bihz'-ih-fy) v. To be active without regard to accomplishments. Some teachers, for example, survive the school day by assigning "busywork" to students which keeps them occupied at their desks, and gives the appearance that learning is taking place. The prime purpose of bizzification in schools is to cover the teacher who is not prepared, or who is in need of time to fill out front-office forms.

bladderate (blad'-er-ate) v. To drag out or prolong a meeting until it must be adjourned to accommodate the physical needs of the participants. Bladderation is often used by those in charge of political caucuses, faculty meetings, association or corporate board meetings, or legislative hearings. Bladderators in charge of meetings usually arrange long coffee breaks prior to the vote which they withhold until people will do anything to get out of the room.

bloatate (blow'-tate) v. An inelegant verb used to denote the expansion or puffing of a report. In practice, many bureaucrats use bloatate interchangeably with trashify. Bloatating produces bloatum, the pappetry of puff pieces, but trashifying merely collects irrelevant materials while producing nothing. Pappetry is the tapestry of bloatated puffery.

bloatum (blow'-tuhm) n. A collective noun used to denote the product of bloatating. Bloatum should not be confused with floatum, a free-floating idea or concept that swirls in search of a safe or meaningful place to land.

blockstone (blok'-stone) v. To bring things to a halt by combining the skills of blockheads and stone-wallers.

boobidoodle (boo'-bee-dood-dl) n. A specialized type of nonsensical doodle drawn by boobidoodlators during boring staff meetings, professional or technical conferences, or committee meetings. Boobidoodles usually reflect the boobiness of the presentation, not necessarily the boobiness of the boobidoodlator. Lawyers use a variant of boobidoodles to encode their billable hours.

boobilate (boo'bihl-ate) -v- (1) To perform a stupid or foolish act. (2) To convert a reasonable thought or act into one that is stupid or foolish. An executive may boobilate by going on a TV talk show without proper preparation.

A politician may boobilate by using vulgar language on radio or by accepting a bribe on camera.

Boren Dictum: If you're going to be a phoney, be sincere about it. (It should be noted that phoney is spelled with an e . . . in keeping with the retrospelling of the ancients.)

Boren Guidelines:
When in charge, ponder.
When in trouble, delegate.
When in doubt, mumble.

Boren Question: Are you willing to bet your entire career (or future) on this decision?

brayality (bray'-al-ih-tee) n. A marginal comment or minimal message that is characterized by loud and resonant braying. Brayalities are heard frequently during political campaigns, but they are also common in commencement addresses, broadcasts of sporting events, and the haranguing pleas of moneyvangelists. (Illustration: His brayalities are threateningly inspirational and money-effective.)

bunkerfy (bunk'-er-fie) v. (1)To build a protective fortification of paper, red tape, in-boxes, out-boxes, computers, filing cabinets, desks and other office materials for the purpose of protecting one's job. A bureaucratic bunker-fication is the institutional counterpart of a military bunker. (2) The staff, the party hacks, and the collective people-barriers who isolate a politician from direct contact of plain, ordinary, people who are not a part of the in-crowd of cronies.

bureaucrat (byoo'-row-krat) n. Once defined as an employee of a governmental agency. Now defined to include anyone who is dedicated to the principles of dynamic inaction, decision postponement, vertical and linear mumbling, bold irresolution, and procedural abstractions. Bureaucracy no longer refers to a workplace; it is a way of life.

bureauphonic (byoo'-row-fawn'-ikh) adj. A word describing the acoustics of the bureaucratic way of life. The bureauphonic approach is more tonal than mental. Similar to but not identical to falphonic entonations, the falacious phonics of engrasping pitches.

bureaustatic (byoo'-row-sta'-tihk) adj. A condition in which the status quo is maximized into a static position while presenting the image of progress.

-C-

cacotone (kah'-ko-ton) v. To speak in harsh and unpleasant tones. The words of a cacotoner may be pleasant in themselves, but the intoning quality of cacotones may grate on the nerves of the listener to the point that the listeners tune out to what is being said. Some senior level executives cacotone without knowing it, while others may purposely cacotone while gradually developing and presenting an unpleasant message. This permits the executive to deliver bad news with a minimum of disruptive reaction from the audience.

cattify (kat'-ih-fy) v. To land on one's feet like a cat. Some cattifiers land lightly and soundlessly on their feet while other thrump and squall as a warning against being disturbed in the future. Cattifiers tend to survive major reorganizations, changes in administration, and complex power plays.

cellumental (sell'-yoo-ment'-tl) adj. A word used to describe the product of a single-cell or shallow mind. A cellumental proposal, for example, is a weak proposal made by a person who is thinking with minimal output but with total capacity. See also monomental and slushmental.

clunkate (klun'-kate) -v- To slide downward or to fall with a resounding finality. Clunkation is failure-oriented. (Adjectival variants are clunkational, clunkal)

coallusion (ko'-aloo'-shun) n. An alliance for a deceitful purpose. Coallusion is a word form that combines the worst elements of collusion with the best elements of coalition. Coallusion is not a Borenword, but was used in Minnesota by a member of Congress, and suggested to me by former Senator and presidential candidate Eugene J. McCarthy. It is a word now worthy of wide usage.

compone (kohm-pon') v. To postpone a decision or an action by referring the matter to a committee.

compuflush (kohn'pyoo-flush) v. (1)To change an embarrassing or otherwise undesirable (fraudulent) transaction by the use of a temporary modification or permanent projection. Compuflushing is an excellent way to lose files through a downspouted drainality. (2) A customer may be compuflushed by lies about the computer being down. Used by hotels which have overbooked and airlines which have lost reservations.

cootle (koo'tl) n. The chortle of an old coot. Cootling coots are not necessarily old coots. Many young coots have ossified outlooks whereas many older coots have creative outlooks.

corbu (kohr'boo) n. Corporate bureaucrat.

-D-

defconsex (dehf'-cahn-sex) -n- Group sex as practiced by defense contractors upon the public . . . with the Congress serving as the budgetary or Red Ink Pimpernell.

diddlematic (didhdl'mah'tihk) adj. A pattern of behavior, automatic in nature, by which a person extracts himself from an unpleasant situation by diddling someone else. Diddlematics can involve automatic transfer of responsibility, an immediate disclosure of privileged information, or any other automatic reaction that assures problem extraction and career survival by blame transference.

dittoanalysis (dih'toe-ahn-ah'-lissihs) n. A pre-Limbaugh term; a special analysis in which previous reports, old conversations, or cocktail party data are presented to support foregone conclusions or weak positions. Dittoanalysis is the analytical tool of echosultants, and is often used by marbleheads.

doodlate (doo'-dl-ate) v. To doodle with professional skill. In terms of thought processes, doodlations can be classified as boobidoodles or thinkidoodles. Many effective executives make use of their time in boring committee meetings to doodlate thinkidoodles that can evolve into major policies, resolve significant problems, or restructure organizations.

drivelate (drih'-vehl-ate) v. To produce drivel with professional eloquence; to express a stupid thought in the form of a profound statement.

dumpromise (duhm'-pro-mize) (1) -v-To arrive at a phoney compromise in which the dominant force dumps on the lesser force. (2) -n- The result of dumpromising.

-E-

echosult (ehk'-o-sult) v. To tell a client what the client already knows, and to do so in the terms the client wants to hear. (One of the reasons that national and state capitals tend to have lower unemployment rates than other cities is the people who are unemployed or "between" jobs call themselves consultants and practice echosultancy.) Print shops specializing in cards and letterheads thrive in capital cities.

econemia (ehk'-o-nee'-meeah) -n- A weak or anemic economy

enflag (ehn-flag') -v- To wrap oneself or some issue in the state or national flag. Enflagging is used to establish one's patriotism or to engoosate an issue into a state of national security.

egoflect (eego-flehkt) -v- To genuflect and make other physical gestures and tonal expressions of subservience that stroke, massage, and otherwise inflate the ego of the person to whom the egoflection is being directed.

engasseate (ehn-gas'-ee-ate) -v- To fill a proposal or expand a speech with valueless gas. Engasseations can provide the needed timality stretch for speeches devoid of ideas.

engoosate (ehn-goos'-ate) -v- To prod with a directional orientation. Engoosations may be physical or psychological nudge. As an expression, engoosation is socially more acceptable than goosing though they share the same root.

engrasp (ehn-grass'-puh) -v- To roughly execute a full grabbality or yanking grasp to capture everything of value that may be within an extended reach. Engraspations are incautious and forceful seizures.

ensugarate (ehn-shoo'-ger-ate) v. To sweeten up a sour policy or position to make it more palatable to the public. Ensugaration may be accomplished through beautiful words, meaningless but publicized awards, appropriately selected and carefully timed expenditure of public funds, and other goods and services.

estroppelate (es-trahp'-pul-ate) v. To prevent a lawyer in a state of rage from contradicting his or own previous assertions. Estroppelate is a functional and conceptual blending of estoppel (a legal term for a restraint on a person to prevent him or her from contradicting a previous statement) and oestrus (a non-human mammalian condition of being "in heat" or in a state of sexual excitement). Whereas estoppel can relate to any person, estroppelate applies only to lawyers. The estrosity factor is to prevent lawyers from doing to each other what they often do to clients.

ethicate (eth'-ih-kate) v. To give an improper or unethical practice the appearance of being ethical. A common ethicating technique is the use of well-known and respected people to serve as character witnesses for unethical practitioners.

exfritterature (ehx-friht'-er-ih-tchoor) n. A type of expenditure in which funds or other resources are frittered away.

- f -

factalysis (fak-tah'-lih-sis) n. An analysis of facts made for the specific purpose of determining which facts should be withheld and which facts should be revealed. Faulty factalysis has resulted in the fall of high level political leaders, purchasing agents, wayward spouses, and con men.

fauxtegrity (fah-teg'-rah-tee) -n- Phoney integrity.

featherheading (feh'-ther-heh'-ding) n. Management overload as expressed in the practice of payrolling more management or senior level staff employees than are needed. Featherheading is used to avoid firing people who should be fired but who are retained on the payroll as an easy way out of difficult personnel situations. Downsizing rarely has any impact on featherheading.

fiddlestrate (fih'-dl-strate) v. To orchestrate something with an emphasis on the variations rather than the theme. A fiddlestrated proposal, for example, is one which fiddlestraddles issue and focuses on marginal thoughts. Fiddlestrators gather in large numbers at conferences of educators, ecumenical gatherings, political conventions, and meetings of talk show hosts.

flackistic (flak-ehr-iss'-tick) -adj- Term used to describe the artistry, skills, and techniques used by public relations specialists whose function is to make the boss appear less ignorant that he or she may be. The suffix "-istic" denotes purposefulness. Therefore flackistic is purposeful flackery. Most flacks, the practitioners of flackery, have ulcers.

flapperator (fla'-per-ay-ter) n. A wheeler-dealer who initiates and thrives on organizational flaps. Flapperators usually have sensitive antenna that can receive and measure institutional vibrations for the purpose of translating them into career opportunities.

flattergast (flat'-ter'ghast) v. To overwhelm someone with flattery.

Most flattergasters are also effective egoflectors, but flattergastery requires less skill and less finesse in its execution.

floatum (flow'-tuhm) n. Bubble-headed, free-floating ideas or marginal concepts that float around conference tables, board rooms, and legislative halls in search of some significant meaning to which they can become attached. Like soap bubbles, floatum flows with the wind and tends to rise and swirl during heated exchanges.

folicy (fahl'-ih-see) n. A fallacious policy. Folicies are often described in fuzzifications which tend to be accepted with little or no question.

frumpate (fruhm'-pate) v. To convert something that is attractive into something that is frumpily unattractive. An executive (or the speechwriter) can frumpate a presentation with cacatonal words or grumples to discourage others from wanting to meddle in the program. Frumpation is often used to protect one's domain.

fudget (fuhd'-jeht) n. A fudged budget. Fudgets are commonly used by politicians, bureaucrats, and executives to build into budget proposals a substantial amount of fiscal fat that can be trimmed without damage to a program.

fuzzify (fuhz'ih-fie) -v- To present information in a manner that is obtuse but seems to be clear and precise but which permits wide adjustivity of present or future interpretation.

- G -

globate (glow'-bate) -v- To deal with the biggest of the big pictures . . . a global approach. In globalities, there are no corners into which the globator can be backed. The higher up a person can bubble in a hierarchy, the more he or she can globate. High level globators deal only in generalities and they need not know the details or the nittygritty of the business. Lower level employees never globate, and they are the only ones who need to know what they are talking about. Politicians are professional globators.

goosality (goo-sowl'-eh-tee) -n- A polite term for the act of goosing. Goosalities and engoosalities are interchangeable terms.

gotchadata (gawt'chuh-date-uh) -n- Information, data, photographs or other unquestioned proof of a charge or claim being made by the gotchadatafier, the developer or owner of the data. Gotchadata is used to inspire someone to do or say what the gotachadatafier wants.

grabbality (grabb-al'-ih-tee) -n- The act of implementing a quick and rough grasp of something. In politics, the term is often used to describe transpalmations of cash.

greedocracy (gree-dawk'-ruh-see) -n- Government by greed.

- H -

halljog (hawl'-jawg) -v- To carry a file folder high under one arm as one moves with great speed, apparent determination, and high visibility through the halls and corridors of one's place of employment. Halljogging impresses superiors and associates with the assumed competence and importance of the halljogger. The technique can be extended to inter-building movement when opportunities present themselves. One should never halljog with a briefcase, because it projects the wrong image . . . that one is arriving late or leaving early.

hunkerfy (hun'-ker-fie) -v- To mentally crouch or shift into a psychological stance and to be ready to leap into whatever direction the hunkerfier believes may be best for his or her career. Hunkerfication is initiated with a state of mental neutrality.

hydropinion (hy'drow-pihn-yuhn) -n- A watered-down opinion that is expressed by a shy or weak-kneed person who wishes to avoid controversy.

- I -

idiotoxic (ih'deeoh-tox'-ihk) -adj- A policy, program, or activity that is toxic or dangerous because of the idiocy on which it is based.

Politicians often use idiotoxicities in series as they express their views or justify their positions on issues.

inframental (ihn'-frah-mehn-tl) - adj- Below the level of mental functioning. An inframental decision or policy can be one based on a hunch or a gut feeling rather than on intellectual evaluation of pertinent factors.

interdigitate (ihn-ter-didg-uh-tate) -v- To interface the digital elements of the hands in a professional manner. Unprofessionally called finger tapping, interdigitation can be executed with either simultaneous or sequential interfacing of the fingers.

intervoid (ihn'ter-voyd) -v- To avoid confrontation; interface avoidance. To some wordologists, the syllabic elements of intervoid may seem to indicate the state of being between two voids. In politics and bureaucracy, this is no inconsistency since the practice of voidal sandwiching is quite common.

intralateralize (ihn-trah-la'-tehr-a-lyze) -v- To make a quiet shift to the right or the left. Intralateral movements are usually minor adjustments made within an organization to assure unity of position and harmony of operation. A management as well as a political practice.

irrelevate (ih-rehl'-eh-vate) -v- To use irrelevant quotes, statistics, and other material: (1) to elevate a discourse to a level of assumed intellectuality, (2) to add supportive bulk and fiber to a non-thinker's diet, or (3) to quantify marginal abstractions and enhance the image of expertise.

isticity (ihz-tiss'-uh-tee) -suffix- The Boren concept of communicating purposefulness through the use of the siffix "istic". Thus, mumblistic refers to purposeful mumbling, not accidental or random mumbling. Putteristic, purposeful puttering; engoosistic, purposeful engoosation; shufflistic, purposeful shuffling. Television moneyvangelists are whinistic as they whiningly beg for money.

- J -

judicopp (joo-dih-kopp') -v- To make a decision in a court of law based not on justice but on the desire to clear the docket. Judicopping is "justice" through copping a plea. It is a judicial tool that taps repeat offenders and hammers innocent citizens who cannot afford to prove their innocence through the court system. Pro bono cases are usually judicopped without consideration of probable innocence or guilt.

- L -

legalate (lee'-guhl-ate) -v- Operating within the technicalities of the law but outside the spirit of the law, legalators stress the image of legality without worrying about the substance. Legalating judges are frequently judicoppers, for example, and are quick to release confessed perpetrators of major crimes for minor technicalities.

legalay (lee'guhl-ay) -v- To delay a decision or action in an organization by requiring an opinion from a lawyer. It buys time for the referring authority while also presenting an image of prudent management. Common in the Congress.

legaldetox (lee'-guhl-dee-tox) -v- To teach managers or administrators who are former lawyers how to stop thinking like lawyers.

loopate (loo'-pate) -v- To avoid the truth or the appearance of truth by slithering outside the loop of involvement.

loopistic (loo-pihs'-tihk) -adj. Denotes a lawyer's purposeful search for, or development of, loopholes through which to pull a client to legal escape, usually in criminal cases. Loopistic is not used to describe the money-oriented loopholes in legislative proposals which lobbyists design for clients.

- M -

maxillate (max'-ihl-ate) -v- To professionally jawbone. To maxillate an issue until the essential elements of an issue are forgotten. Practiced in political gatherings, courtrooms, graduate level seminars, association board meetings, and Congressional hearings. In forensic terms, maxillation is jawbonal stretch.

mindclot (mynd'-klawt) -n- A sudden stoppage in the flow of thoughts. Mindclot can result from boredom, sleepiness, and the replacement of thinking processes by the impactions of televised idiotoxicities.

molarcheck (moe'-lehr-chehk) -v- To count or explore one's molars (uppers and lowers) with the tongue. Molarchecking is commonly used as an aid to staying awake in staff meetings, lectures, church services, and banquets.

moneyvangelist (muhn-ee-van'-gee-list) -n- Money-oriented evangelists who measure the power of their messages by: (1) the flow of cash offerings, and (2) the degree to which they can tilt the political axis to fit their personal political agenda. Genuine religious experiences are based on the sincerity of the victims who give their money, not the subsincerity of the moneyvangelists who prey by pitching and praying.

monomemo (moh-no-mehm'-oh) -n- A memorandum that deals with a single subject. Rarely seen in operational bureaucracies.

monomental (moh-no-mehn'-tuhl) -adj- An adjective used to describe the product of a one-track mind.

Mount Hokum (Mount-Hoh'-kuhm) -n- Capitol Hill in Washington, or Parliament Hill in Ottawa.

mousify (mou'-suh-fie) -v- (1) To respond mousily to a political or a business management problem --- a skittering away with fearful withdrawal. (2) To hesitantly and mumblingly accede to a proposal that one does not like.

multisyllabattic (muhl-tih-sill-uh-battick) -adj- The forceful interfacing of multisyllabic words. Multisyllabic words flow; multisylabattic words boom and pop.

mumbella (muhm-beh'-luh) -n- A musical term denoting unaccompanied mumbling.

mumblesce (muhm-bless') -v- To mumble with resonant and poetic overtones.

mumblio ad libitum (muhm-blee-oh add' lih-biht'-uhm) -n- Frequently used as a note used by speechwriters to instruct speech makers to fill gaps or stretch the speech by randomized mumbling.

mumblio cum plinkus (muhm-blee-oh come plihn'-kus) -n- A mumble that does not ring true, or one that has the plink of a counterfeit mumble.

mumblio in vacuo (muhm-blee-oh inn vack-yooo-oh) -n- An empty mumble. It is an interstitial mumble that is not a connective tissue with any other mumble.

mumblio infra dignitatem
(muhm-blee-oh ihn-frah dihg-nih-ta-tehm) -n- A mumble that is beneath one's dignity or is unworthy of one's rank.

mumblio obbligato (muhm-blee-oh oh-blee-gah'-toe) -n- Required mumbling. Usually a marginal note used as an instruction to a speechmaker. It may be a short part of a long oratorical score . . .such as a sermon, a commencement address, or a public official's review of his or her record.

mumblio ostinato (muhm-blee-oh ose-tee-naw-toe) -n- A constantly recurring mumble in a speech that usually carries elusive fragments of a thought. In politics, used by speechwriters to remind the speaker of the subject being discussed. Particularly useful at the end of a speech so the speaker can conclude more or less back on the subject.

- N -

nincompoopify (nihn-kawm-poop'- ih-fie) -v- Anyone can oopsify a minor mistake, but only a nincompoop can nincompoopify. Nincompoopification can be the pooping off of money or other resources in governmental agencies, academe, religious institutions, or legislative bodies. Nincompoopery is a life style; nincompoopification is a management practice.

- O -

onstop (awn'-stawp) -v- To continue the process of a stoppage . . . usually at a constant rate of stoppage. Onstopping programs are similar to ongoing programs except the continuity is in the stopping instead of going.

oopsify (oop-sih-fie) -v- To commit a minor mistake.

- P -

pompistrut (pawm'-pihs-truht) -v- To move about with optimal pomposity.Usually practiced with the stomach pulled in and the bridge of the nose held approximately parallel to the floor. Some politicians and bureaucrats can appear to be pompistrutting while seated. Pompistrutting can be observed in theaters, at diplomatic receptions, or political dinners.

poppalities (pawp-al-uh-tees) -n- The sounds of bursting bubbles. Some politicians speak with poppalities . . . particularly when speaking into microphones.

posicator (po'-zih-kay-tore) -n- A person who is a professional poser of comments in the form of questions. Posicators are found in political gatherings, caucuses, educational conferences, and neighborhood condominium meetings.

positosity (paw-zih-taw'-sih-tee) - n- A firmly held position based on information or assumptions that are full of holes. Positosity is a position-porosity interface.

potamale (pah'-tah-mah-lee) -n- A di$h of political cornpone developed in the Valley of the Potomac; a mixture of fiscal mush generously laced with expensive pork; wrapped in corn shucks; served with vote-getting brayalities.

profundify (pro-foon'-deh-fie) -v- To make simple ideas seem profound through the use of multisyllabic wordalities and tonal solemnity. Profundifications are thesaurus-enriched.

prostiposit (prahs'-teh-paw-sit) - v- To take a position on an issue or problem in return for money, privileges, promotions, travel, or other rewards.

- Q -

quobble (quaw'-bl) -v- To raise a relevant question or make a significant statement about something important. Quobbling is the opposite of quibbling.

- R -

residuate (ree-sihd-yoo-ate) -v- To move into a fixed, immovable position while maintaining a very low profile. Residuation is often a survival practice used during periods of crises, changes of management, and downsizing.

retroanalyze (reh'-trow-anowl-lize) -n- A special analysis of past failures or unhappy events for the purpose of finding a scapegoat. A political mainstay.

retropunt (reh'-trow-puhnt) (1) - n- To implement a kickback. As in retropuntal funding. (2) -n- A kickback, as in to receive a retropunt. Developed as a Borenword during the author's service as a consultant to a law firm who sought an intervoidal term to extricate a client from a difficult situation.

rostrate (raw'-strate) -v- To thunderate from a rostrum in a manner that optimizes flourishes and tonal patterns while minimizing the transfer of information. Politicians, moneyvangelists, media pundits, and trial lawyers are noted rostrators.

rumperatory (ruhm'-per-a-tor-ee) -adj- A descriptive word applicable to the laggistic element of bodily structures, logical abstractions, and other posteriorities. Rumperatory statements reflect the rumbleseat or afterthought of bureaucratic or political wisdom. Rumperatory abandon describes the way most men think and a few women walk.

- S -

scratchalities (skrat-chal'-uh-ees) (n) Cash, bonds, contracts, and other things of value. A broader form of scratch (money).

scurrency (sker'-ehn-see) -n- Currency that is fast-moving during rapid inflation-deflation spiralizatons. Scurrencies scurry about the financial landscape of countries whose monetary policies are determined by votes rather than economic factors.

sheepal (shee'-puhl) -adj- (1) sheep-like behavior; (2) a poetic term for the politicians' treatment of a gullible public.

showl (shh-owl') -v- To project a pattern of high-speed shouting and howling. Though occasionally used by politicians, showling is primarily the communicative style of moneyvangelists, automobile dealers, and furniture stores.

sinceriphonics (sin-seer-uh-fawn'-icks) -n- The sounds of sincerity used to cover phoniness. Often theotonal in nature.

sleazality (slee-zowl'-uh-tee) Cheap, smelly, chauvinist, or racist material that are gutter oriented. Most often a poluttal factor during political campaigns.

slushmental (slush-minh'-tuhl) -adj- Sloppy-minded thinking.

snortation (snohr-tay'-shun) -n-

An oratorical gasp that stresses a sequence of thundering inhalations and challenging grunts.

snuggery (snugh'-ehr-ee) -n- A place, usually hidden, where various interests can be brought together for warm, comfortable and mutual advantage. In politics and bureaucracy, snuggeries are used as the hatching centers for the development of new policies to ultimately harass taxpayers.

Spendagon (spin'-dah-gawn) -n- The taxpayers' name for the Pentagon. A center where numbers are crunched for the development of the federal fudget.

squaggle (squaw'-guhl) -v- To move randomly with slow serpent-like progression.

- T -

taxcoma (taks-ko'-muh) -n- A state of unconsciousness suffered by a taxpayer who is hit by a sudden and overwhelming tax burden.

taxxes (taks'-ehz) -n- An extended system of taxes that axes creativity, and taxes the productive abililty of an individual or organi-

zation. Taxxes reach farther and hit harder that simple taxes. The Value Added Tax is a taxx.

theotonal (thee-oh-tohn'-uhl) - adj- The whinal tones of money-vangelists begging for money. Often borrowed as a communicative tool by politicians who have lost an election or who are under investigation.

thinkidoodle (thihnk'-ee-doo-dl) - n- A specialized doodle that is doodled when a person is thinking.

thunderate (thun'-der-ate) -v- To speak in loud and roaring tones. Thunderators are known for the force of their roar and the vacuuity of their messages.

toadality (toe-dowl'-uh-tee) -n- A word, action or other expression by which a toady expresses his or her toadiness. Toadality is an expression of the supreme subservience of one individual to another.

translateralize (tranz-latt'-ehr-uhl-lize) -v- To move something from one place to another with such skill that the change is accepted without question.

transpalm (tranz-pawlm) -v- To transfer cash or other things of value from one palm to another. Transpalmation is today's primary motivational approach to legislative action. In politics, transpalmed cash is the essence of a meaningful handshake.

- W -

winesop (wine'-sawp) -n- A person whose knowledge of wine is surpassed by a pretentious and boring babble of expertise. Winesops, for example, babble about wines that "caress the tongue while being firm to the palate" and "offer a lovely nose . . . a bouquet of fruity excitement and ambrosial joy." Secretly, if give a choice, many winesops would choose a beer or a chocolate milkshake over a glass of tongue-caressing wine.

- Z -

zilchify (zihlch'-ih-fie) -v- (I) To do nothing. (2) To convert something of value into something of no value.

PART SIX.

Epilogue

The Mountain Top and the Sunrise

How do you reach the Mountain Top in politics? Is there one to reach? Or, should you continually strive to stumble, stomp, and kick your way up what you perceive as the next rung of the political ladder? Are there significant differences between the Mountain Top of rare air and the Deep Valleys of flushing waters? Do you have the proper balance of ego and humility to see you through some of the swamps you must wade before reaching the base of the mountain? These are only a few of the ponderables that one must consider if one is to feel a great sense of satisfaction from all the struggles of political life.

Assume that by using the strategies and minimal lessons learned from this book you have reached what most hacks, flacks, and philosophers declare to be the top of the mountain. What do you see as you view the political landscape from the lofty view? Were all the tense moments, the lack of sleep, the cost of personal treasure, the wrenching pains in the gut, and the Punctured Back Attack worth it all? What do you see?

Do you gaze upon smog-filled valleys rising above the wetlands and swamps? Do you smell the foul odor of the hog waste, the chicken litter, the paper mills and the chemical plants that pollute the rivers and lakes as they churn out profits for the polluting companies? Do you see people . . . just plain, ordinary, citizens . . . hurrying about the valleys and the mountains trying to develop ways of cleaning up the environment? Or, do you see evidence of a great fog of apathy gradually smothering all the world's living creatures and plants in the extractive industry of greed? Do you see a land where once-assumed freedoms have given way to increased governmental intrusions into peoples' lives? A society willing to

191

give up individual freedoms for the promise of less crime and more security? A society where the police power is officially privatized, and the rich and powerful protected from the growing rumblings of the poor and weak?

Come, now, that's enough of pessimism! Let us be optimistic!

Let us look over the valleys and plains at a land where an invigorated people whip off the blanket of apathy, and decide to regain control of their own government. Let us smile as we see bright, young leaders with enthusiasm, purpose, and love of freedom rising toward the mountain top . . . with a determination to lift our nation to the heights where once again we will find honesty, decency, and justice for all. Let us see our great land with its temporarily slumbering people take the lead in non-military persuasion in international affairs. Let us see our nation spending every dollar spent for war-making being matched by ten dollars for education, health, and well-being of all our people from babyhood to the twilight years. How exciting! What a wonderful way of life we can find again when we reject the people-eating policies of the greedocracy that has thrived in the abyss that apathy made possible! From the Mountain Top . . . let us see the sunrise of hope . . . a bright and shining future.

Up and at it, folks! There's work to be done . . . to re-write this book as a story of public servants serving the public.